Challenges to Communism

Challenges to Communism

John G. Gurley

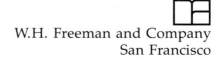

W.H. Freeman and Company
San Francisco

This book was published originally as part
of *The Portable Stanford*, a series of books
published by the Stanford Alumni
Association, Stanford, California.

Library of Congress Cataloging in Publication Data

Gurley, John G.
    Challenges to communism.

    Reprint. Originally published: Stanford, Calif. :
Stanford Alumni Association, 1982.
    Bibliography: p.
    Includes index.
    1. Communism.   2. Communism—History.   3. Capitalism.
4. World politics—1945–   .   I. Title.
HX73.G87   1983   335.43   83-1471
ISBN 0-7167-1506-6
ISBN 0-7167-1507-4 (pbk.)

Printed in the United States of America

1 2 3 4 5 6 7 8 9 0 MP 1 0 8 9 8 7 6 5 4 3

This book is dedicated to

Cynthia Fry Gunn

who for almost ten years edited and managed the Portable
Stanford series with the highest professional standards and
integrity, with consummate skill, and with more care and
devotion than anyone had a right to expect.

CONTENTS

PREFACE

DURING 1974 AND 1975, it was becoming obvious to many people that a startling change had occurred in the fortunes of the major capitalist countries. Their growth rates were sliding; inflation was rising; unemployment, imbalances of international finances, lagging capital formation, and other economic problems were accumulating; the OPEC cartel had exhibited its power; and the loss of the Vietnam War had diminished the ability of the United States to prevent the further global spread of communism. In 1975, I addressed these issues in *Challengers to Capitalism: Marx, Lenin, and Mao*, my first book in The Portable Stanford series. I was principally occupied in that work with Marxism and the ways it had contributed to the weakening of the capitalist world.

Since that time, I have become increasingly aware of the reverse relationship: the impact of capitalism on the communist world. Communist countries have declined economically since the early 1970s, partly because of the slowing growth of capitalist economies but largely because of their own internal problems. However, upon close examination we see that these internal problems of the communist nations have also been strongly shaped by capitalism's own historical patterns of development.

This book, *Challenges to Communism*, addresses chiefly the many intricate ways that capitalism over more than a century has crafted the main features of the present-day communist world. Capitalism not only produced Marxism, but it drove this revolutionary movement from the more advanced areas of the capitalist world and sent it scurrying into the less-developed areas, where Marxism ever since has been pounded this way and that by the hammer blows of capitalist societies. As a result of these attacks and of its own internal problems, world communism now appears to be in the beginning stages of a long-term decline.

This book also carries forward the theme of my earlier work, namely that communism, in many important respects, has weakened the present-day capitalist countries. Each of these two giants, capitalism and communism, although armed to the teeth, now confronts the other in economic and social disarray. There is an emerging third figure in the picture, however, the rising world of the developing countries—the so-called Third World—which is dramatically involved in the ongoing contest between capitalism and communism. As the arguments develop, it is my hope that the reader will better understand the force that each of the three worlds has exerted on the others.

The closing chapter marks my effort to pull the threads of these arguments together to set forth what I regard to be the most likely prospects for each of the three worlds; the chapter pays special attention to the possible fate of communism.

This book is written for both the general reader and students in economics and political science courses. It can be used in studies of comparative economic systems, economic development, Marxism and Communism, and international relations. It may also be useful as supplementary reading in more general courses, such as beginning economics or political science.

I am indebted to my present luncheon companions and former teachers, Bernard F. Haley and Edward S. Shaw, for the exemplary models they have provided me over the years. Elizabeth Campbell's editorial assistance was invaluable throughout the production of this book. Cynthia Fry Gunn, my editor, to whom this book is dedicated, performed as she has always performed, with rare intelligence, sound advice, and a warmth that was not always justified by my own performance. To my old teachers and my new ones, I offer my thanks.

John G. Gurley

Stanford, California
December 15, 1982

Top: Armored personnel carriers rolling through Moscow's Red Square in November 1982 during the celebration of the sixty-fifth anniversary of the Bolshevik Revolution. (UPI) Bottom: Hundreds of Poles assembled in Warsaw in May 1982, bearing Solidarity banners and shouting "Gestapo" and "Free Walesa." (Sygma)

1

The Many Faces of Communism

COMMUNISM IN THE WORLD TODAY offers us many views of itself, any one of which, taken alone, is incomplete—even incompatible with others. Consequently, as we observe this "creature" from various sides, we become ever more perplexed about its true nature.

Views of Communism

One view suggests that communism is a strong revolutionary movement throughout the Third World of underdeveloped countries. It has achieved victories in China, Cuba, Mozambique, Vietnam, Albania, and more than a dozen other countries. Partly in response to this view, the U.S. government has poured billions of dollars into rapid deployment forces and other weapons, into economic and military aid to vulnerable regions, and into other supports to sustain anticommunist regimes around the world. This view reveals communism as a decided menace to capitalism and democracy.

However, if we observe communism from another vantage point, it appears to be on its last legs. This perception presents the Soviet Union and virtually all of Eastern Europe in an economic quagmire, bogged down with grossly inefficient productive facilities, recalcitrant workers, heavy foreign debts, planning systems in shambles, and shoddy consumer goods. The economies of other communist countries, such as Cuba, North Korea, Angola, and Vietnam, are foundering, too. Few of them are able to feed their people. It is this view of communism that led President Reagan to declare before the British Parliament that the Soviet Union and other communist countries are in such deep economic difficulty that the West can reasonably plan and hope to see Marxism-Leninism left on the "ash heap of history"—a prognosis that came at the very time when the U.S. military budget was being greatly enlarged to meet the communist danger.

1

This apparent contradiction can be resolved not only by invoking these two opposing views but also by noting still another visage of this strange creature, namely that it possesses, through the Soviet Union, a nuclear-weapons arsenal that could wipe out much of the world in a few minutes. From this viewpoint, to say that communism has great strength in the world today is a gross understatement. The Soviet Union's status as a military superpower easily rivals that of the United States. It is this view of communism that helps to account for the vast military expansion by the United States, as well as for continuing anxieties in the West over what the Soviets might do next.

But we can swing to the other side again by viewing communism through its internal fracases—through its descent from a fairly cohesive international movement to a fragmented lot of quarreling and discordant nations. China has regarded the Soviet Union as enemy number one, and the Soviets themselves have amassed troops and armament along the Chinese borders. For its part, China has invaded Marxist Vietnam with substantial military forces. Yugoslavia and the Soviet Union, Albania and the rest of Eastern Europe, Cuba and China, the Soviets and the Hungarians and then the Czechoslovakians—all have been at odds with one another. Even the communist parties of Western Europe find cooperation with one another difficult, and each has some sort of complaint against either the Soviet Union or China—and sometimes against both. This view certainly discloses communism as a weak international force, a movement that appears to be bringing about its own destruction.

Still, if we move to yet another angle, communism can suddenly appear once again as a *force majeure*, in that it possesses a most powerful critique of capitalism, which has appealed decade after decade to hundreds of millions of disadvantaged peoples throughout the world. A major part of this critique is Marxism's analysis of the exploitative nature of capitalism as a global system. This has aroused nationalist and left-wing fervor against foreign capitalists, their multinational corporations, and their values and culture. The theories of Marxism-Leninism have fed these fires of rebellion and turned many in the world against the alleged agents of imperialism and neocolonialism. Communism's censure of "exploitative capitalist society" has hit home among the world's impoverished in ways that capitalist ideology has not been able to match. This advantage has been pressed even further by communists' presentation of socialism and communism as a set of ideals. These ideals, rather than the actualities of communist regimes, have mobilized the energies of many poor peoples for the attainment of a more just society.

We have not yet exhausted the many faces of communism. If we view this movement through its early stages, strong economic achievements cannot be denied. From the late 1920s to Hitler's invasion in 1941, the

Soviet Union, albeit at great human cost, transformed an economically backward society into a major industrial nation—almost, it seems, overnight. The Chinese communists, too, made remarkable economic progress during the 1950s, the first decade of their development efforts, by establishing a base of heavy industry and a vast network of light industries, many of them in the countryside, and by mobilizing human labor and traditional tools and opening up new land to boost agricultural output far above pre-1949 levels. Although the economic growth rates in both of these countries have faltered over the past few decades, the initial accomplishments of the Soviets and the Chinese continue to inspire people of other nations and thereby to impart strength to communist movements.

Again, however, we can move to other positions and see communism as little more than a weak sister. For one thing, it has made virtually no headway in the advanced capitalist countries, despite Marx's prediction that proletarian revolutions would occur first in precisely those countries. Revolutionary Marxism has been especially weak in several of the major capitalist nations—the United States, Great Britain, and West Germany—and it has little presence throughout northern Europe, Canada, Australia, and elsewhere. Although communism is a force to reckon with in France and Italy and to a lesser extent in Japan, even in these countries the communist parties have modified considerably their revolutionary stance and seem more willing to accept and work within democratic institutions than they once were. Communism as a revolutionary movement in the advanced capitalist countries cannot now be taken very seriously.

Moreover, in the underdeveloped areas where it has come to power, communism has largely failed to produce socialist societies that have succeeded in capturing the admiration of any sizable number of people. Many more people over time try to leave these societies than knock on their doors. Marxist culture, democratic processes, and opportunities for human fulfillment in communist countries have not lived up to the expectations of the founders of communism. Marx and Engels and many of their followers fully anticipated a brilliant era of communism lying beyond socialism, but the Marxist regimes have offered only rapidly diminishing prospects of such an era. For those who are sensitive to the shattering of these ideals, communism appears as a much weakened force in the world.

So communism does have many faces. Our judgment of it depends very much on which face, or faces, we are looking at. These faces, which reflect for the most part the actualities of the communist movement, have their counterparts in the intricacies of Marxist-Leninist theory, for that theory is at once a critique of capitalism, an indictment of imperialism, an analysis of socialist economic development, a recipe for revolution against capitalism, and much else. The theory has influenced the actual practice of communism, and the practice in turn has induced revisions in the theory. This interaction between theory and practice is itself part of Marxist analysis—that part which sets out to explain how knowledge of the real world is acquired. The actual communist movement, therefore, is largely incomprehensible in the absence of an understanding of Marxist-Leninist theory. The essential elements of this theory are presented, in summary fashion, in the pages that now follow.

The Marxism of Marx and Engels

Marxism, as originally formulated by Karl Marx (1818–1883) and Friedrich Engels (1820–1895) in the mid-nineteenth century, comprised four main elements:

1. A theory of history that revealed capitalism to be transitory;
2. An analysis of capitalist production that showed labor to be exploited by capital;
3. An analysis of the capital accumulation or growth process that concluded that capitalism creates both wealth and poverty and, for this and other reasons, is subject to periodic crises; and
4. A theory of proletarian revolutions that alleged the inevitable victory of socialism in advanced capitalist countries.

Theory of History

We shall discuss Marx's and Engels' theory of history in the next chapter; here it is sufficient to note that these authors studied how feudalism was succeeded by capitalism and then postulated that capitalism would be followed, first, by socialism and, then, by communism. Further, their theory specified that each of these societies would carry the seeds of its own destruction. Their theory did not predict beyond communism, for that mode of production still lay too far into the future for sufficient evidence to be brought to bear on that question.

Marx and Engels considered socialism to be a transition between capitalism and communism, and as such it would contain many remnants of the former society as well as the buds of the next era's flora. Socialism would be, they believed, a society transcending capitalism although still a class society—one with a dominant working class but also subordinate former ruling classes and other less important groupings. The stage beyond this would usher in the classless, affluent society of communism.

Strictly speaking, therefore, there are no "communist" countries in the world today, for the nations so called are in fact still, at best, in the socialist transition stage. Nonetheless, we shall use "communist" to reflect both the aspirations of these countries and the names of their own political parties. The distinction between socialism and communism is examined more thoroughly in Chapter 2.

Theory of Exploitation

The next two elements of Marxism, as originally formulated, relate to the essential mechanisms of the capitalist system. The first of these asserts that, although the working classes produce the total value of goods and services, using the machinery and buildings that they themselves have also produced, a capital-owning class appropriates part of this value. Capitalists purchase "labor power" at its value, which is the value required to maintain the current workers and to provide for the next generation of workers, but capitalists receive the value of "labor," which is the output produced by workers and which exceeds the value of "labor power." Capitalists pocket the difference—which Marx called "surplus value"—because they own the capital goods, control the production process, and acquire the commodities produced by the workers. Because of these positions of power, the capitalists enforce a working day on the laboring class that exceeds in length that which is necessary to maintain and reproduce the workers. Surplus value (profits, interest, rent) is to Marxists the measure of capitalists' exploitation of the laboring class.

Periodic Crises

Marxism also asserts that capitalism produces business cycles of ever-greater magnitude and that they are necessary for the survival of capitalism—though in the end they will help to destroy it. In Marxist analysis, periodic crises are basically caused by too much wealth in capitalists' hands and too much poverty among the proletariat: The former leads recurringly to excessive capital formation (i.e., too many investments in capital equipment, structures, and inventories) and so to falling rates of profit, owing to excessive capital goods relative to the supply of labor in the production process. The low incomes of the working class result in such low levels of consumption expenditures that continuing high rates of capital formation become unprofitable.

These periodic downturns weaken labor more than owners of capital. They idle many workers, creating excess supplies of labor and so lowering wages. At the same time they also depreciate much of the value of capital goods as demand for them declines. This lowered value establishes the conditions for higher rates of return on capital in the future. The economic downswings also provide opportunities for the stronger capitalists to buy these lower-valued capital goods from capitalists in distress, thereby concentrating capital in fewer, more powerful hands and eliminating much competition. These developments reverse the trends that build up against capital during the prosperity phases, and so capitalists become poised for another upswing of capital accumulation.

Marxists have taught their followers over many decades to consider mass unemployment and hard times as normal and necessary occurrences of capitalism, which can be eliminated only by socialist planning.

Proletarian Revolutions

The fourth proposition of Marxism is that successful proletarian revolutions will occur first in the most advanced areas of capitalism, during one of capitalism's ever-more-severe crises when the urban working class will have had time, through a series of class struggles, to mobilize its forces and to gain an understanding of itself as a class, of the source of its problems, and of the revolutionary solutions to these problems. Therefore, according to Marx and Engels, socialism would be able to succeed only a capitalist society that had developed fully on both the capital and the labor sides, producing ever-more-concentrated and vulnerable wealth, on the one hand, and ever-more-mobilized and class-conscious poverty, on the other.

In fact, twentieth-century socialist revolutions have occurred, not in the advanced areas of capitalism, but in the less-developed regions of the world. They have taken place in Russia, China, other parts of Asia, here and there in Africa and Latin America. Even before this century began, it had already become obvious to many Marxists that proletarian revolutions in Western Europe and North America were most unlikely. Such revelations led some European Marxists to advocate a more evolutionary road to socialism and communism, a road that utilized the democratic institutions of Europe and America. These theoretical explorations and the accumulation of further information generated by capitalism's course during the last half of the nineteenth century provided the Russian communist leader, Vladimir Ilyich Ulyanov (1870–1924), known by his pen name of Lenin, with sufficient material to revise and extend Marxism into what later became known as Marxism-Leninism.

Marxism-Leninism

This body of doctrine consists of Marx's and Engels' original theses plus a series of later propositions. Lenin contributed the following two theories:

5. A theory of monopoly capitalism and imperialism that explained how capitalism in the latter half of the nineteenth century developed into a world system, with an advanced "center" dominating and exploiting lesser imperialist countries and all of them extracting wealth from the poorer, colonial areas of the system; and

6. A theory of revolutions and communist parties in the less-developed, colonial areas of the world-capitalist system that explains how the people of the poor nations, with the aid of a vanguard communist party, could overcome imperialism.

Imperialism and Dependency

The fifth component of Marxism-Leninism alleges that capitalism developed, as Marx predicted, from a stage in which enterprises were small, numerous, and competitive to a stage in which capital became highly concentrated in a relatively few giant corporations (industrial and financial)—a stage that Marxists term "monopoly capitalism." This analysis contends that these huge enterprises, beginning around 1870, extracted so much surplus value from their domestic activities that, if it were all used at home for capital formation, rates of profit accruing to the capitalists would have declined to unacceptable levels. Increasing amounts of the surplus value had to be exported to underdeveloped areas, where they were employed in mining, manufacturing, agriculture, railroad building, and construction of port facilities, earning much higher rates of profits, which Lenin called "superprofits." When some of these superprofits were returned home, they boosted the economic growth of the home countries, and therefore enabled at least part of the working classes to attain higher standards of living. Thus, the profitability of colonial imperialism to the advanced center of world capitalism aided in reducing the radical tendencies of workers there and so contributed to the transformation of revolutionary Marxism into a more gradualist, reformist movement in the center.

Lenin and later Marxists have added to this picture. They have stressed that the advanced countries redesigned the economies of the peripheral areas in ways that served the interests of the center but often disadvantaged the poor countries—for example, by turning some of these economies into mere suppliers of raw materials to the industrial nations, others into areas for the colonization of white settlers, and still others into outlets for the manufactured goods of the center—the last reducing the poor countries' opportunities to develop industrial sectors of their own. In these ways, the growth potential of the colonial areas was frequently stunted or distorted, and many of the workers and peasants found their futures not only dim but dependent on the whim of foreigners—through their multinational corporations, their discriminatory trade policies, and their powerful financial arms. These areas became, as a result, more vulnerable to working-class revolutions; they became the weakest links in the world-capitalist order. Accordingly, revolutionary Marxism moved out of the advanced center and became rooted in the more impoverished lands.

Revolutions in the Third World

The sixth element of Marxism-Leninism was necessary because of the different and more complex class structures generated in the underdeveloped areas compared with the simple polarity that Marxists expected in the advanced center of capitalism—the bourgeoisie on one side, the urban

Тов. Ленин ОЧИЩАЕТ землю от нечисти.

A Bolshevik poster depicting Lenin sweeping away capitalists, kings, and high officials. (New York Public Library Picture Collection)

proletariat on the other. The stunted and distorted growth in the peripheral areas meant similar disturbances to their class structures. Instead of developing large capitalist and working classes, as had the advanced capitalist nations, these underdeveloped areas found themselves with a small and immature class of local capitalists, many peasants, a group of powerful landlords, few urban industrial workers, a large number of small capital owners (the petty bourgeoisie), and the increasing presence of dominating foreign capitalists.

The first problem that faced Lenin and his successors was how to fashion from the more progressive units of the different classes a revolutionary force that could topple the existing autocratic regimes and the ruling classes that the regimes supported. These initial revolutionary movements could utilize the cause of nationalism against imperialism, the demand of urban laborers for improvements in their terms and conditions of work, the desire of peasants for their deliverance from landlords and for claims to their own land, the demands of many for broader democratic rights, and the desire of local ("national") capitalists to cast off their subservience to foreign ("international") capitalists.

Once this initial revolutionary wave succeeded, the second problem was how to refashion a revolutionary force that would carry the movement past its democratic, nationalistic stage onward to socialism. This required the mobilization of the even more radical elements of workers and peasants who would revolt against the bourgeoisie and the private property institutions within which the bourgeoisie thrived.

Lenin and his successors thus conceived the revolutionary drive toward socialism—from the starting points of autocracy and mass poverty—to occur in two stages, and with substantially more complications along the way than in the relatively simple revolutionary scenario envisaged by Marx and Engels for Western Europe and North America.

Because of these complications and the need to mobilize people into a revolutionary force, Lenin proposed a vanguard communist party that would be composed of professional revolutionaries in a tightly knit and secretive organization. This party's task was to lead the revolutionary forces to victory and, afterward, to guide the entire country toward socialism and communism. For Marx and Engels, communist parties were integral parts of working-class movements, the leaders and members of which were workers. For Lenin, by contrast, such a party consisted of Marxist intellectuals with knowledge of socialism and was formed apart from the workers, whose concerns principally revolved around wages and working conditions. The party was to impart socialism to the workers and become their real vanguard unit.

Socialist Economic Development

Lenin did not live long enough after the Russian Revolution to contribute importantly to the determination of how to achieve a socialist economic society after the proletarian revolution had been won. But other Marxist theorists and practitioners have addressed this problem, and have thereby provided the seventh and final component of Marxism-Leninism:

7. A theory of economic development that explained how relatively poor countries could attain socialism.

This topic was, at the beginning, molded in discussions among Soviet economists during the 1920s, strongly revamped in practice by Joseph Stalin (1879–1953) during the 1930s and 1940s, modified substantially by Mao Zedong (1893–1976) starting in the late 1950s, and revised and extended since then by numerous other Marxists. Most of these contributors would agree that the goals of Marxist development are to achieve much higher standards of living for the masses and at the same time to promote socialist values and socialist institutions.

One basic problem is whether the Marxist country should first build up its productive capabilities before transforming its institutions to socialist forms, or the reverse. Conceivably, at some additional cost, both tasks could be attempted concurrently. Other problems are whether, in building up production, the emphasis should be placed on heavy industry (producers' goods), light industry (consumers' goods), or agriculture; on production for domestic use or for exports; on small, labor-intensive industries or on large, capital-intensive operations; on material work incentives and thus on sizable wage disparities or on greater equality of incomes; and so on.

Marxism-Leninism today offers a variety of answers to these and similar questions about socialist development, for actual experience has been quite diverse. For example, Stalin's strategy, which emphasized a heavy industrial base, was vigorously disputed by Mao, who advocated a more balanced effort between industry and agriculture. Fidel Castro in Cuba has vacillated in his approaches to development, North Korea is developing along more centrally directed lines than is Hungary, and Yugoslavian development features enterprises owned and managed by workers, unlike the situation in Bulgaria, China, and most other Marxist countries. (We shall return to these problems in Chapter 6.)

Just as communism has many faces, Marxist-Leninist theory, too, has multiple facets. Communism is the practice of Marxist-Leninist theory; the latter is bent and reshaped by the experiences of the former. Both have been modified by the world in which they have developed, and that world itself may be viewed from any number of perspectives.

The "Worlds" of the World

There are several helpful ways of grouping the nations of the world for purposes of economic and political analysis. We read about the West and the East, the North and the South, the rich and the poor, and the First, Second, Third, and Fourth worlds.

Although these terms are variously employed, the West generally refers to the industrial countries of Western Europe, North America, and Japan (sometimes Australia, New Zealand, Israel, and South Africa are included as well), whereas the East comprises the Soviet bloc and China. The West, therefore, is composed of the advanced capitalist nations, while the East is made up of the major communist countries. (The East could also be construed to include Mongolia, North Korea, and the communist countries of Southeast Asia.)

The North generally includes the wealthier nations of the globe, whatever type of economic system they have, and the South refers to the earth's poorer countries, again regardless of type of economic system. Accordingly, the North comprises the countries of the West as well as the Soviet Union and the wealthier countries of Eastern Europe. The South is meant to cover southern Asia, Africa, and Latin America—however, the wealthier countries of these regions are sometimes excluded.

The classification of countries into rich and poor is generally done in terms of national income per capita. Those countries with very high per capita incomes, regardless of their geographical location, are placed in the first category, and those with very low per capita incomes, wherever they are located, are grouped as poor. Middle categories between these two extremes are often used, too.

In the final classification scheme, the First World is essentially the West—the advanced capitalist countries. The Second World includes all of the communist countries—that is, the East plus the communist countries of southern Asia, Africa, and Latin America. All of the other countries of the world, which are the noncommunist less-developed nations, are grouped into the Third World. However, the Third World is sometimes divided further into the oil-producing-and-exporting countries—such as Saudi Arabia, Kuwait, and Nigeria—and all the others. Hence, we sometimes hear of the Third and Fourth worlds, the latter being the poor nations.

Marxists are usually reluctant to identify a Third World as consisting of noncommunist less-developed nations, for they see most of these nations as underdeveloped capitalist ones, tied in closely to the First World as subordinates of dominant powers. That is, the standard Marxist view is that there are basically only two worlds, one of world capitalism and the other of world communism, each structured hierarchically.

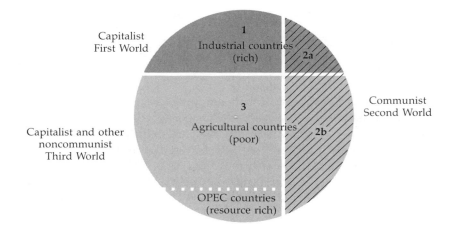

Mao Zedong, however, had quite a different conception of reality. For Mao, the First World consisted of the two superpowers, the United States and the Soviet Union. The Second World was made up of the wealthier capitalist *and* communist countries (which Mao did not recognize as being truly socialist or communist), and the Third World consisted of the poorer capitalist and communist nations, including China itself. This dramatically different vision of the world was based on Mao's analysis that there was no longer a socialist or communist camp, that some form of capitalism had been restored in the Soviet Union and in Eastern Europe, and that China, almost alone, represented the Marxist blueprint of a socialist society. Thus, Mao saw the world around him as essentially a capitalist one, divided into the rich and the poor, with China identifying itself with the latter.

This book for the most part adopts the usual three-world scheme, which is illustrated in the drawing above. In this presentation, the globe is first divided into the rich industrial (areas 1 and 2a) and the poor agricultural (areas 2b and 3) nations. Each of these two groups is then divided into capitalist or noncommunist (areas 1 and 3) and communist countries (areas 2a and 2b). The First World comprises the capitalist industrial nations, shown in area 1. The Second World includes areas 2a and 2b, while the Third World is in area 3. The drawing also shows separately within area 3 the Organization of Petroleum Exporting Countries (OPEC), because its great oil wealth sets it apart from the others. If this division is made, the oil-rich countries, and perhaps a few others, would comprise the Third World, and the Fourth World would be made up of the remainder—the truly poor.

In the beginning years of this century the world approximated being only one world—a capitalist world of rich dominant and poor subordinate nations. Beginning with the Russian Revolution of 1917, a Second World began to take shape, leaving the huge remainder more sharply defined as a First World. After World War II, when the less-developed capitalist and other noncommunist countries gained political independence from their former colonial masters, a Third World came into being. This reduced the dimensions of the First World, confining it to the wealthier capitalist countries.

None of the three worlds is monolithic; in each there are serious doctrinal differences, sometimes manifested in opposing armies. But the view of this book is that capitalism and communism are essentially different, each profoundly affecting the other, and that both of these camps have strong impacts on Third World countries—and vice versa. These interactions and their consequences are the subject of what follows in the pages to come.

A Bolshevik poster echoing Marx and Engels' call that the workers "have nothing to lose but their chains and they will gain the whole world." (New York Public Library Picture Collection)

2

The Marxist Meaning of Socialism and Communism

MARXISM IS, IN PART, A THEORY about social transformations. As Marxists see it, in the world today socialism is in the process of succeeding capitalism, just as capitalism overcame European feudalism several centuries ago. Socialism, Marxists believe, will eventually usher an entirely new era into the world, a socialist era that in turn will be followed by a communist one. Marxism, as we have seen, is more than a theory, however. It is also a real revolutionary movement throughout much of the world, a movement that is attempting to create the socialist societies, and ultimately the communist systems, contained in the theory.

The Development of Socialist Thought

Early Meaning of Socialism

The word *socialism* was first used in its modern sense in November 1827 in the *Co-operative Magazine,* a London publication of the followers of Robert Owen; and it appeared in a French periodical a few years later. For the Owenites, "socialism" meant a system of mutual cooperation, the opposite of self-love, which leads to individual competition, and it also meant the common or social ownership of capital goods. "Socialists" in those days, as in ours, were the enemies of individualism and of laissez faire and were in favor of collective organizations based on planning and on cooperation among individuals. They had no faith in any natural law, such as the "invisible hand" of competition that was supposed to reconcile automatically the self-seeking of individuals and the welfare of society, and they distrusted the ability and willingness of politicians to remedy societal ills.

From its earliest days, socialism has consisted not only of critiques of capitalism but also of proposals for a better society—socialist blueprints. Some of the early socialists, such as the Welshman Robert Owen (1771–1858) and the Frenchmen Charles Fourier (1772–1837) and Étienne Cabet (1788–1856), founded cooperative communities, such as New Lanark in Scotland and Brook Farm in Massachusetts, to serve as prototypes of the new society. This so-called utopian socialism, which flourished from about 1820 to 1860, consisted of a series of efforts based on the creed that the evils of capitalism can be avoided, and eventually eliminated, through example—by the establishment of model communities in which cooperation and scientific order will produce economic abundance and harmony for all members. Most utopians stressed the need for order to replace the chaos of actual society. Some utopian communities (mostly religious ones) sought escape from the world, but the aim of most secular societies was to influence and change the world. Consequently, utopianism was not entirely, or even largely, escapism. These movements were influenced by Jean-Jacques Rousseau (1712–1778) and other writers of the Enlightenment, who gave currency to the belief that a golden age had existed before its corruption by European civilization. This image of the ideal community of the past was easily carried over to the desire for one in the present.

Later socialists, such as Louis Blanc (1811–1882) and Ferdinand Lassalle (1825–1864), attempted to establish their versions of socialism by legally transforming the institutions of the existing societies into ones more congenial to the working classes. Blanc was a socialist politician and journalist in France, and a forerunner of modern democratic socialism. He became a member of the provisional government of 1848, and after a long exile in England returned to France as a member of the National Assembly in 1871. In his early writing, *Organization of Work* (1839), he advocated the establishment of national workshops by the state, and more generally assigned to the state the key position in economic planning and the development of welfare services. He believed that the state should aid the working class in various ways, but that the workers' associations should be run by the workers (after a year or so of training), not by the state. He wanted to transform the state peacefully into the agent of the working class. Blanc's workshops were to be organized first in industry and then, later, in agriculture (as collectives, combining rural industry); they were to be self-governed, using modern technology, and competitive with private enterprises. He expected that the national workshops would gradually spread and so drive out capitalism entirely. Ferdinand Lassalle was a German socialist and lawyer who championed a type of state socialism in which the state, after universal suffrage had been won, would financially aid the working class in establishing producers' cooperatives, with ownership and control in the hands of the workers.

Other socialists, such as Karl Marx and Friedrich Engels, sought to overthrow the entire capitalist system to pave the way for a socialist society that they saw as the "associated mode of production"—a society of freely associated individuals working with capital goods and land held in common and having a definite social plan, the ruling principle no longer being profit but human needs.

All of these socialists had definite ideas about the societies they wished to see erected alongside of, within, or on the ashes of the capitalist one, which they despised.

The Background of Marxism

Marx and Engels were born in Rhenish Prussia about thirty years after the outbreak of the French Revolution, just a few years after the final defeat of Napoleon, and in the midst of what came to be called the Industrial Revolution.

Marx (1818–1883) was born and grew up in Trier, in the Rhineland, spending the first half of his life in Western Europe studying, writing, engaging in revolutionary activities—and being shunted from one place to another because of them. During the second half of his life he was in and around London, where he went after being banished from Paris, and where he died over three decades later. Two years before going to London, he and Engels wrote the Communist Manifesto. *He spent much of his time in London gathering data against capitalism in the library of the British Museum, and some of this evidence later appeared in his most mature work, volume one of* Das Kapital, *in 1867. Much of his life was also devoted to workers' organizations, political causes, and meetings with revolutionary émigrés. Marx died fifteen months after his wife and was buried next to her in Highgate Cemetery on the outskirts of London.*

Engels (1820–1895) first met Marx in Cologne in 1842 and began collaborating with him a few years later—an intellectual partnership that lasted for almost forty years, until Marx's death. For many of those years, Engels supported the Marx family financially, the funds coming from a Manchester textile business with which Engels was associated. In the very year that Engels was made a partner in this capitalist firm, he helped to establish the International Workingmen's Association—the First International—which was dedicated to the destruction of capitalism. After Marx's death, Engels edited the second and third volumes of Das Kapital, *a task that used up much of his remaining life. His own contributions to Marxism have generally been underestimated, for he wrote many outstanding works in economics, military affairs, philosophy, and history. These contributions are all the more notable inasmuch as he probably sacrificed his own talents to a considerable extent to Marx's own personal needs.*

Engels, in his essay, *Socialism: Utopian and Scientific*, which was written in the late 1870s, alleged that modern socialism was, first of all, the direct product of the Enlightenment—the eighteenth-century intellectual movement in Europe that expressed confidence in human reason and thus in a rational and scientific approach to all problems. This movement, in which Diderot, Voltaire, Rousseau, and Hume played prominent roles, fostered the belief in progress and perfectibility, and it attacked dogmatism, spiritual authority, intolerance, and all other magisterial pronouncements. It advanced the notion that people themselves, acting in harmony with the universal order, could bring about rational progress. The Enlightenment, through its attacks on religion and absolutism and its advocacy of economic reforms and constitutionalism, figured importantly in inciting the French Revolution; and it paved the way directly for Adam Smith's laissez faire doctrines in his *Wealth of Nations* (1776), which marked the advent of classical economics. These movements played their own roles later on in the development of Marxism.

The French Revolution began in 1789. Among its deeper causes was the commercial-capitalist expansion in France during the seventeenth and eighteenth centuries, which greatly enlarged the middle classes and elevated their economic position in the nation. At the same time, however, backward social and political institutions, which confronted the middle classes, frustrated their attempts to translate their economic power into social and political gains. The nobility and clergy ruled France, while, at the bottom of the pyramid, some peasants were still serfs, many more were tenant farmers subject to feudal dues of various types, and most were subject to recurring famines and hard times. Against this background, more immediate factors contributed to the revolution, such as the chaotic state of government finances and the depressed economic conditions at the time, and the intellectuals' forceful attacks on the church and royal absolutism.

The Industrial Revolution refers to the burst of technological innovations that transformed capitalism from its commercial and agricultural phase into its industrial era, with its factory system of large-scale machine production and its assembly of capital and workers in great urban factory centers. This revolution occurred first in Great Britain from about 1750 to 1850, took hold in France and Belgium after 1830, began seriously in Germany after 1850, and captured the United States following its civil war of 1861–65. It later spread to Japan and Russia, and still later to many other countries.

The Industrial Revolution in Great Britain grew out of that country's strong commercial and financial expansion in the preceding decades: rising demands for consumer goods from a growing and wealthier population, early technological advances in the key sectors of energy use and cotton textile production, and the presence at home of large quantities of coal and iron ore deposits. All combined to enable Britain to leap ahead of the rest of the world and to claim industrial supremacy for more than a century.

French workers storming the bastion of capitalism led by Marianne, who has broken their shackles. Lithograph by Steinlin. (The Bettmann Archive, Inc.)

The progress of capitalism in Britain and on the Continent thus produced the Industrial Revolution, which not only enlarged and transformed the bourgeoisie from commercial to industrial capitalists but gave rise to a new class of urban workers, the proletariat, who were propertyless and thrown together in work places and dwellings under excruciating conditions. Also, as already noted, the progress of commercial capitalism in France contributed to the French Revolution, which, with its demands for liberty, equality, and fraternity, in turn inspired and fomented working-class movements in Britain and in much of the rest of Europe. Thus, the development of commercial capitalism was an important precursor of both the Industrial Revolution and the French Revolution, which in turn set the stage for the rise of the industrial bourgeoisie and the revolutionary proletariat—and, hence, for Marxism.

Marxism, as both a theory and a movement, evolved within this revolutionary environment to serve the interests of the urban working class, which was demanding higher wages, better working conditions, shorter hours, limits to child and female labor, and political representation. Marxism was the ideological agent of the proletariat in the same way that the classical economics of Adam Smith, James Mill, David Ricardo, and others ministered to the rising dominance of the manufacturing and industrial business class. Each of the two major classes, then, had its intellectual mentors who defined all of society's purposes and processes in terms of their class's own particular interests.

The Origin of Socialist and Communist Ideas

From the Marxist perspective, the core elements that describe socialism and communism emanate from history itself, from the way people have changed the world through production, progress in science, and participation in class and national conflicts. Now let us examine the key elements of Marxist socialism.

The Marxist View of Socialism

Political power of workers. Ever since the days of Marx, his followers have claimed that there can be no socialism without political power held by the working class. That is, workers must control the state—its executive, legislative, and judicial branches, its armed might, and its bureaucracies. Moreover, many but not all Marxists are persuaded that the state must take the form of the dictatorship of the proletariat—that is, working-class dictatorship over the former ruling classes. In observing history, Marxists find that societies have always been ruled by certain social classes, such as slaveowners, feudal lords and clergy, or landlords and capitalists; moreover, new ruling classes have arisen to overthrow old ruling classes. Given the events of the twentieth century, Marxists see no reason to believe that these power transformations have come to an end. The question then becomes: What class is most likely to displace the current ruling class?

The materialist conception of history. Marx developed a theory about questions like this, which he called the "materialist conception of history." This theory states that quantitative changes (which Marx believed to be inevitable) in the *productive forces* will ultimately cause qualitative changes in the *social relations of production,* usually achieved through revolution, and these changes will sooner or later transform most of the *superstructure.* The italicized phrases require explanation.

The "productive forces" include the material means of production—capital goods and land—and human labor. They develop through the labor and activity that people expend in extracting a living from their natural environment. Part of this development consists of the growth of human abilities and needs, and part consists of progress in technology and science. Thus, during the basic work activity, the society's productive forces expand, and people become increasingly capable of providing for themselves at the same time that they develop needs for ever more provisions.

The "social relations of production" are the institutions and practices most closely associated with the way goods are produced, exchanged, and distributed. They include property relations (who owns what); the way labor is recruited, organized, and compensated; the markets or other means for exchanging the products of labor; and the methods used by the ruling classes to capture and dispose of the surplus product. The social relations of production are, in effect, the class structure of a society that is revealed in the work process. That is, work institutions and practices readily reveal which classes are dominant and which subordinate.

Sooner or later, according to Marx's theory, the developing productive forces come into conflict with the prevailing class structure. The newly developed ways that people extract a living from their natural environment become incompatible with the older ways they relate to one another in the work process. For example, commercial activities, based on the expanding productive forces (capital goods, land, human labor), became incompatible with the feudal relations of production (class structure). This growing contradiction takes the form of a class struggle between the rising class, associated with the new means of production, and the old ruling class, whose dominance was based on its control of the older, waning forces. This class struggle, under appropriate conditions, intensifies the contradiction between the productive forces and the social relations (or, more to the point, between the two classes) until, as a result of revolution, new relations of production are established, which are compatible with the superior productive forces.

Marx termed the combination of the productive forces and the social relations of production the "economic base" of society. He postulated that

The new "Member of the Board." Labor begins to demand its share in industrial management. Drawing by Eduard Thony. (The Bettmann Archive, Inc.)

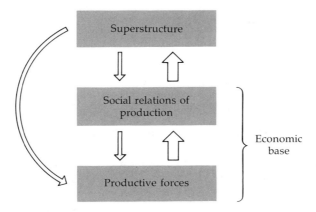

the economic base molds the "superstructure" of social, political, and intellectual life, including individuals' sentiments, morals, illusions, modes of thought, principles, and views of life. The superstructure contains the ideas and systems of authority (political, educational, legal, military) that support the class structure of that society—that is, the dominant position of the ruling class. In brief, how people make a living shapes their mental conceptions and supporting institutions. It follows that the transformation of the economic base eventually causes the character of the superstructure to change.

In Marx's materialist conception of history, the main causal route to this transformation runs from the productive forces to the social relations of production and on to the superstructure. But there are also interactions among the three elements. A successful revolution by one class over another, for example, will eventually cause many of society's leading values to change, but these values in turn will affect the future progress of the productive forces. These interactions are shown in the chart above, in which the wide arrows denote the main causal connections and the narrow ones indicate feedback reactions.

Marx's study of the Industrial Revolution and of other historical events led him to his theory, which pointed to the industrial working class as the revolutionary force that would overthrow the class of capitalists and thereby capture political power. In Marx's day, the industrial workers were growing rapidly in numbers and strength, and Marx reasoned on the basis of what he saw all around him that they would in time arise to topple their exploiters. Marx's successors concurred with this prediction, on the basis of their own studies of social change and of contemporary events. According to Marxists' reading of history, socialism requires the dictatorship of the proletariat because in all class societies the ruling class has prevailed only by such control over the subordinate classes—control that is exercised constitutionally when the ruling class is not threatened but that is imposed overtly and arbitrarily when it is.

Public ownership and economic democracy. Another key element of socialist thought is the public ownership and democratic management of society's material means of production (capital goods and land). To Marx and his followers, history has shown that the retention of political power by a minority ruling class, such as in feudal and capitalist societies, is possible only if that class owns and controls the productive instruments—that is, only if there is *private* ownership. But when the majority of people—the working classes—possess political power, as in socialism, they can retain such power through the *social* ownership of capital goods and land. The working classes could not maintain their control of the state if they did not have control of the productive instruments—that is, if the former ruling class continued to own them privately. In communism, there is only a single class, so there is necessarily public or social ownership, for there is no minority class to claim such rights.

Marxists also believe, from their study of history, that the democracy that has developed over the centuries in many capitalist societies has been limited mainly to the political sphere, and that it can be extended into the economic realm only when socialism succeeds capitalism. This follows from the observation that in capitalism the private ownership and control of the material means of production by the ruling class of capitalists are incompatible with democratic decision making in the work places—for workers cannot be given the power to outvote a narrow group of owners on basic questions involving the capitalists' rights and privileges. But when the working classes own and control the material means of production, more democratic arrangements within work places become possible. As a consequence, socialist programs aim to attain greater economic democracy by allotting wider decision-making powers to the workers, from production problems in the units where they work to planning for economic and social goals in the nation where they live.

Central planning. A third component of socialist thought involves the role of central planning, which in a world of nation-states usually means national planning. Rather than relying on the interplay of individuals' decisions in markets, socialism employs plans developed by technicians. The purpose of this planning is to achieve the economic goals of the society—such as high growth rates, stable prices, and full employment—and to meet the essential needs of the vast majority. Planning for needs is to replace what Marxists consider in capitalism to be the more-or-less anarchic production for profit. The cellular feudal society in Europe precluded national planning, and, in fact, made it impossible for anyone even to conceive of it. Owing to its slow growth without business cycles (which first appeared in the early stages of industrial capitalism), feudalism demanded little in the way of any sort of planning, at whatever level. Central planning in the form of national planning, of course, requires nations, which developed along with capitalism at a later date.

As capitalism developed out of the feudal period, business enterprises and family households became increasingly engaged in buying and selling in markets that were volatile and uncertain, and in using money, credit, and banks—all of which made it necessary for enterprises and households to plan their incomes, expenditures, savings, and indebtedness. Thus, the development of capitalism itself induced a certain amount of microplanning. In addition, the appearance of industrial business cycles in the early 1800s—with their short bursts of prosperity and inflation, followed by periods of growing unemployment, financial crises, and other economic disorders—compelled national governments to engage in at least some minimum amount of macroplanning.

The historical growth of both micro- and macroplanning under capitalism suggested to Marxists and others that planning would have to be extended, and market activity reduced, if the needs of the working classes were to be properly met. In addition, Marxists believe that experience suggests that central planning and nationalized enterprises support one another, in that planning is best carried out by responsive (rather than hostile) enterprises and that publicly owned enterprises can operate more efficiently within overall plans. Because both central planning and publicly owned enterprises diminish the importance of markets and private profit making, they reduce the economic role of capitalists and so contribute to the retention of workers' political power.

Greater economic equality. Still another facet of Marxist socialist thought is that it aims for greater economic equality among the people than is achieved by capitalist societies. This idea emanated from one of the most obvious features of early capitalism: the appearance of harsh inequalities among people, some of whom were making quick, fabulous fortunes but most of whom were caught in grinding poverty and appalling work conditions. The earliest critics of capitalism, such as Thomas Hodgskin (1783–1869), William Thompson (1785–1833), and John Francis Bray (1809–1895), focused on this evil and offered remedies for it. Although many of the worst aspects of inequality have been largely removed since those days, Marxists believe that much economic disparity and even absolute poverty remain in capitalist countries. As a consequence, their socialist programs continue to include critiques of and cures for this social disease.

Marx furnished the basis for the later discussion of this point by emphasizing that the distribution of income and wealth in capitalist societies is largely determined by the distribution of ownership of the means of production. Insofar as these material productive forces are in the hands of a relatively small class of capitalists, the distribution of income is bound to be greatly uneven, too. "Any distribution whatever of the means of consumption," Marx wrote in his *Critique of the Gotha Programme*, "is only a consequence of the distribution of the conditions of production themselves."

To Marx, it followed that income (and consumption) distribution can be made more equal through collective (or working-class) ownership of the means of production. Consequently, the socialist aim of greater economic equality is to be achieved largely through the vehicle of collective owner- ship. This would eliminate the private appropriation of most property income (profits, rent, and interest), placing such income in the state budget ("in the hands of the people," as socialists see it) for uses that benefit the society in general. Since property incomes are fairly large and highly con- centrated in capitalist countries, collective ownership would go a long way toward equalizing standards of living.

Socialists also propose to achieve greater economic equality through the narrowing of wage and salary differentials (consistent, however, with the maintenance of work incentives), the discouragement of gambling and of speculation on commodity and financial markets, and tighter restrictions on passing private estates forward to the next generation.

By all these means, socialists intend to build greater equity into the economic system rather than achieve equity goals, as capitalist societies do, by ad hoc measures involving taxation, welfare, and regulation—that is, by corrective measures superimposed on a system that generates ine- qualities in its mode of operation.

These four core elements of socialism are components of Marx's relations of production and the superstructure. Two other core elements exist as well, one of which relates to the forces of production and the other to communism, the stage beyond socialism.

Enlarged productive forces. The fifth element is that socialism seeks to build up its forces of production so as to attain high standards of living for its citizens. This notion is derived from the economic progress that has marked the world over the past two centuries, as exemplified by capitalism's greater economic achievements compared with those of its predecessors. Marxists' optimistic conviction of economic improvement over the long term is also incorporated, as we have seen, in Marx's materialist conception of history. By extending the historical record through capitalism and into the socialist era, Marxists expect that socialism will exceed capitalism's performance.

Momentum toward communism. Finally, Marxists believe that a socialist society must preserve a momentum toward the future classless society of communism. This belief in communism is based on the inference from historical processes that working classes will achieve political power, and that, inasmuch as they represent the great majority of the population, they will not be successfully challenged by yet another class. In time, therefore, class societies will disappear.

The Marxist View of Communism

In Marxist thought, communism, the stage beyond socialism, is characterized not only by its classlessness and its material abundance but also by the distribution of this abundance according to people's needs rather than in conformity with their work contributions. From what has previously been said, the derivation of the first two notions is clear. The last one is based on Marxists' observations regarding income distribution in various types of economic societies. The distribution of income in slave societies was arbitrarily and largely made according to whether one owned slaves or was a slave—that is, according to owner-owned relationships. Later, under feudalism, income distribution was based predominantly on the relations of people to the land—whether they owned and controlled it or simply had some rights, as serfs, to work on it. During the capitalist era, income distribution has been made according to ownership (of capital goods and land) and work skills and efforts. Marxists have extrapolated these historical experiences into a socialist era, in which the distribution of income is expected to be based largely on work performance but to some small, though increasing, extent on the basic needs of individuals.

As Marxists see the historical picture, income has always been distributed, partially and haphazardly, according to the needs of some of the people—if only for the purpose of pacifying them. Such a distribution principle has been extended under capitalism, but, Marxists believe, more as a way of correcting abuses of the system than as a positive principle. The principle of needs is expected to become increasingly important during the socialist era and to become the ruling guideline under communism.

Reshaping the Core Elements

Because the core elements of socialism and communism emerge from historical events in the material world, they have been reshaped over time as the world has changed. For example, Marxists have lowered the living standards that are consistent with the concept of socialism as working-class revolutions have spread among the world's poor. Thus, the Chinese Communist party declared China to be a socialist country in 1956, only seven years after the revolution, when its income per capita for the first time exceeded levels previously attained in China, even though that income was still barely above subsistence levels.

The success of Marxism in the underdeveloped areas of the world has led some Marxists to postulate a transitional stage between presocialism and socialism. Leon Trotsky (1879–1940), for example, believed that the Soviet Union, even during the 1930s, was not yet a socialist society, but rather "a preparatory regime transitional from capitalism to socialism." He grounded this view on the low level of that country's productive forces, arguing that state and collective ownership of the means of production do not necessarily mean socialism, for such juridical forms may indicate bureaucratic control of capital goods, land, and labor at low levels of national income but working-class control at higher levels of national income—when workers are prepared to exert such control. Although other Marxists feel differently about this particular point, most of them have come to see a need for envisaging some type of transitional period, inasmuch as socialism cannot be expected to emerge immediately after the working classes have acquired political power in more-or-less impoverished countries.

Technological advances and additional development experiences have also altered conceptions of central planning. Computers, for example, have raised the potential effectiveness of such planning. However, actual experience with planning in present-day socialist countries has revealed many difficulties and inefficiencies and thus has suggested a more decentralized structure of planning, or more reliance on markets in conjunction with production plans.

As socialism has reached more deeply into peasant societies, "political control by the working class" has come to mean different things. It once meant that the urban industrial workers would directly assume political control, but today, in the light of additional experience, it indicates control by communist parties that have predominantly peasant members. In the same way, "public ownership of the means of production" has acquired new forms and combinations, such as rural communes in China and worker-managed enterprises in Yugoslavia. This socialist term now comprises a wider assortment of types of publicly owned enterprises than it once did.

During the 1920s and 1930s, Stalin and other leaders of the Soviet Union sometimes spoke as though socialism would be very quickly followed by communism. Similarly, during the Great Leap Forward in China, 1958–59, Mao Zedong stated that his country was only a few years away from entering the promised land of communism. In both cases, such high hopes turned into bitter disappointments. As a result of these and similar experiences, communism is now generally thought of as lying further in the future and as more difficult to attain than was once believed.

Secondary Conceptions of Socialism and Communism

Although the core elements of socialism and communism have been reshaped from time to time, they are shared by most Marxists throughout the world because their experiences and their observations of world-historical processes have been more or less similar. But there are many secondary conceptions of socialism and communism that come from the special cultural traditions and experiences of particular peoples, and hence are held almost exclusively by them. These secondary conceptions are the principal reason for our awareness of the diversity of types of socialism in various parts of the world.

In Maoist China, for example, during the period 1949–76, the path to socialism was punctuated by "leaps," in which social relations of production were radically changed within a short period. In Stalinist Russia, 1928–53, the socialist path was marked by many unbalanced priorities—industry favored over agriculture, huge projects over small ones, urban workers over peasants, producer goods over consumer goods, and so on. The Soviet Union has many more state farms than does China, and Poland relies heavily on private farming. The Albanians have pursued self-reliant policies more diligently than have the Czechs, who have counted much more on foreign trade and credits to spur their economic growth.

Thus, socialism is both a universal and a local product. In large measure, it is a product spawned by capitalism itself as well as by the traditions and special characteristics of each of the countries involved.

Theory versus Practice

There are often gaps of various dimensions separating the conceptions of Marxists about socialism and communism and the realities of socialist societies. But, as previously noted, many of the conceptions themselves have changed over time in accordance with new experiences and accumulating evidence. Moreover, Marxists often have wide differences of opinion among themselves about socialism and communism—differences that arise from their varying interpretations of world-historical processes and from varying traditions and cultures that are found from one nation to another.

Nevertheless, there is a tendency among Marxists to cling to notions of socialism and communism that are no longer supported by compelling evidence, a failing that is found in many groups. However, we must be continually aware throughout these pages of possible differences between theory and practice. Whereas this chapter has been largely devoted to the theory of socialism and communism, later chapters will focus strongly on the actual performances of Marxist and capitalist societies.

A German syndicalist poster produced by the International Workers Association proclaiming that "the freeing of the working class must be the work of the workers themselves!" (Mueller and Graeff Collection, Hoover Institution Archives)

3

The Failure of Communism in Western Europe and America

MARXISM, AS A THEORY AND A REVOLUTIONARY MOVEMENT, grew out of the particular ways that capitalism developed. Capitalism in Western Europe produced not only Marxism but many of its rivals as well, both in Europe and America, and by so doing helped to neutralize this chief revolutionary threat against the capitalist order. In the process of industrial growth, capitalism also generated commercial and financial problems that captured the focus of working-class movements for a number of decades, deflecting them from central and more revolutionary aspects of Marxism. A variety of other forces converged as well to enfeeble the revolutionary Marxist movements in the advanced areas of capitalism. In the end, revolutionary Marxism was tamed, caged, and declawed. Here we shall examine closely the failure of communism in the advanced nations of the world, where Marxism became little more than a caricature of what it once promised itself to be.

The Failure of Revolutionary Marxism

Revolutionary Marxism specifies that the development of capitalism will produce an industrial working class which, at an appropriate time, will carry out a successful revolution against the capitalist class and then, with the aid of the dictatorship of the proletariat, will establish first a socialist society and ultimately a communist one.

Although as a theory revolutionary Marxism was born in the late 1840s, as a practical movement it did not begin to take hold until Marx played an important role in establishing the International Workingmen's Association in London in 1864. Even then, this First International was dominated, most of the time, by other groups. After that, the practice of revolutionary

Marxism appeared faintly in Germany only after 1875, weakly in France toward the end of the nineteenth century, hardly at all in Great Britain, and with little force in the United States. However, it did appear with some strength in Russia near the turn of this century. European workers' organizations were sometimes committed to revolutionary Marxism in theory but seldom in practice. Thus, the movement was very slow in getting started, and even when it was finally under way its outlook quickly changed from revolution against capitalism and its democratic institutions to reform of capitalism within these institutions. Revolutionary Marxism triumphed only outside of what Marx considered its proper surroundings.

The objective revolutionary potential of the working classes throughout much of Western Europe rose during the first several decades of the nineteenth century, perhaps reaching a peak between 1840 and 1870 and declining thereafter. It was during the 1840–70 period that the critical variables influencing this revolutionary potential were all pointing in the revolutionary direction: a rapidly rising number of workers dependent on wages, the beginning of labor organizations and a growing awareness among the workers of their common problems, a sharp diminution in crafts and an equally rapid rise in largely unskilled and homogeneous labor, an intensely exploited labor force working long hours under poor conditions and without adequate access to political institutions for redress, and growing disparities between rich and poor. After 1870, the objective revolutionary potential of the working classes declined as the further growth of capitalist economies created many new skilled jobs and an increasingly diversified labor force, with expanding service, technical, professional, and scientific work opportunities and a contracting blue-collar production sector. Moreover, the struggles of workers, their growing union strength, and the interests of capital as a whole compelled state action to raise the health and training of the labor force. All of these factors elevated workers' standards of living, provided peaceful political outlets for their grievances, made them much less class conscious, and, as the American Marxist Paul Sweezy has said, turned "a potentially revolutionary proletariat into an actual reformist force."

Moreover, during the period when the objective revolutionary potential of industrial workers was at its peak, the revolutionary theory of Marxism was largely unknown or misunderstood by the working classes and hence was of little help in guiding them to a revolutionary solution to their problems. That is to say, the subjective element of the revolutionary situation was not favorable at the very time that the objective conditions were propitious. Critical variables influencing the extent to which communism was accepted by the working classes included their basic understanding of the theory, their participation in struggles against capital, the degree to which they could identify themselves with Marxism's goals and strategies, and the competing ideologies demanding their attention. After revolutionary Marxism was accepted, or at least understood, by large segments of the working classes, if only in theory, the objective conditions for revolution were no longer favorable.

The growing presence of ideologies competing with revolutionary Marxism played a crucial role in diverting workers' attention from a potentially powerful and useful theory, and it is to these rival theories that we now turn.

The Rivals of Revolutionary Marxism

The earliest attacks on industrial capitalism, which predate socialist thought, concerned some of the wrenching changes from conditions that presumably existed in previous societies—that is, in those societies that were simpler, more rural and agricultural, and more religious. Some of the shocking features of early industrial capitalism were the blatant inequalities among people, the competitiveness and greediness that seemed to possess more and more poor souls, and the increasing dominance of urban-industrial over rural-farming life with its concomitant disruption of family structures, abusive use of child labor, and the existence of miserable living and working conditions.

Rousseau and the Utopians

The initial denouncers of late-commercial and early-industrial capitalism, such as Rousseau, Owen, Fourier, and Cabet, concentrated on these evils, ascribing them mostly to the rise of commerce, industry, and speculation, and to the institution of private property. Not being able to see solutions to these evils in the future development of capitalism itself, these early critics offered other remedies or escapes: back to Nature—by returning to the simple, uncorrupted life; back to God—through the religious regeneration of mankind; or flight into oases of justice—through the establishment of model communities set apart from the surrounding wicked society. In this early period, it was understandably much easier for these invokers of censure to visualize a step or two backward into a better life than it was to see any answer beyond the present that would be achieved by the continued progress of the existing society.

The French social philosopher Charles Fourier, for example, one of the outstanding utopians of his day, criticized the hypocrisy and deceit of his society, and its tendency to make everyone natural enemies. The Scottish economic historian Alexander Gray, in his book The Socialist Tradition, *has Fourier asserting that civilization is "an endless morass of mess, inefficiency, swindling, and lying—a sewer in which every human relationship is poisoned and warped." Fourier sought efficiency and harmony in place of the wastefulness of unrestrained individualism. He detested industrialism and so advocated a back-to-the-land policy—a return to small communities ("phalanxes") com-*

bining agriculture and small-scale manufacturing in which, however, unequal living conditions and private property played their roles. His method was not political agitation, labor organization, or revolutionary forays, but withdrawal into a model community that would rally an increasing number of people in similar communities to the good cause, and ultimately demonstrate to the world the desirability of such living arrangements.

In his phalanx or model community, as Fourier imagined it, all work was done on a cooperative plan—communal kitchens, a communal granary, communal nurseries and schools—which would allow women to work alongside men and would substantially raise the efficiency of work and, hence, the wealth of the community. Indeed, the main purpose of the phalanx was to replace wastefulness with efficiency, not to achieve justice or equality, for within and without the community were shareholders, and the members could be quite rich or relatively poor in their private possessions. Even the meals prepared in the communal kitchens would reflect such inequality, for some were lavish and others quite modest, priced accordingly. The essence of Fourierism was planning, order, harmony, association, and cooperation; attractive, dignified, and enjoyable work; and efficiency.

In America, the propagator of Fourier's ideas was Albert Brisbane (1809–1890), social theorist and newspaper columnist, whose book Social Destiny of Man (1840), an exposition and commentary on Fourier's system, was a smashing success. Horace Greeley (1811–1872), editor and founder of the New York Tribune, who was later the Liberal Republican and Democratic parties' choice for president of the United States, also supported Fourier and gave space in his newspaper to Brisbane for this purpose. Many phalanxes (perhaps forty to fifty) were founded in this country in the 1840s and 1850s. One of the first was at Red Bank, New Jersey, established in 1843 and devoted primarily to agriculture. Another was at Brook Farm, West Roxbury, Massachusetts, which set out to substitute a system of brotherly cooperation for one of selfish competition. They were all failures, though their lifetimes varied from a month or so to twelve years. By the time of the Civil War, Fourierism had run its course.

It was actually the early "progress" of capitalism that created in the first place the complaints against it. This progress entailed the disruption of traditional conditions, values, and institutions, and at the same time it created, for many people, offensive new relationships. Voices were raised against the attending evils of the new society, and solutions were sought outside of the capitalist system. As we have seen, for many decades, utopian thinking exerted powerful influences on many dissenters, turning their minds back to a supposed golden age despoiled by civilization. Later in the nineteenth century, Friedrich Engels decried this "mishmash" of half-baked nostrums, which for several decades led many workers down blind alleys. From such mishmash, wrote Engels in Socialism: Utopian and Scientific, "Nothing could come but a kind of eclectic, average socialism, which, as a matter of fact, has up to the present time [1880] dominated the minds of most of the socialist workers in France and England." In this fashion, utopian thought seeped into the body of revolutionary Marxism like a poison, weakening its penetration into the ranks of the urban poor.

Movements Using or Reforming the Capitalist State

During much of the nineteenth century, the state in Western European countries came to represent broader interests politically; the right to vote was extended to more adults; trade unions were officially recognized and their demands given some attention; parliamentary reforms were carried out that widened effective representation; and commoners continued to gain political power vis-à-vis the nobility and the monarch. These trends were most marked in the north: Britain, the Netherlands, and the Scandinavian countries; less so in the south: France, Italy, Spain, and Portugal.

Thus, in the nineteenth century the state became increasingly involved in the political life of the nation. Moreover, toward the latter part of the century, the transformation of industrial capitalism from small, numerous, and competitive enterprises to much larger and more market-dominating ones (the latter often called, by Marxists, the stage of "monopoly capitalism") produced new waves of empire building, greatly strengthening the economic, as well as the military and political, roles of the state. In the twentieth century, the trend of increasing state involvement has accelerated dramatically, as manifested, for example, in the steep rise of government activity in the production and distribution of the gross national product.

In any event, the state was a force to be reckoned with throughout much of the nineteenth century, and critics of capitalism confronted it in various ways. Some wanted to ignore or at least to bypass the state as they drove toward the new society; many of the utopian socialists and the "cooperators" held this ground. The latter were members of the cooperative movement, which got under way in Great Britain during the 1830s and 1840s. The movement was an integral part of trade unions, which established cooperatives for production so as to employ their own members and threaten employers with the loss of their business. Consumer cooperatives were also founded, many dealing in the products of producer cooperatives.

Other critics of capitalism proposed to make use of the state for their own purposes: to reform it (the British Chartists); to get financing from it (Louis Blanc and Ferdinand Lassalle and their followers); or to transform it into a socialist instrument (the British Fabians and the reformist Marxists). Still other critics desired to displace or overthrow the state. These movements, other than revolutionary Marxism, were anarchism, syndicalism, and guild socialism.

Chartism was a movement in Great Britain to extend the franchise and to reform Parliament with the immediate aim of increasing the political power and in the long run the economic welfare of workers and other disadvantaged groups. However, while economic discontent lay behind the political demands, the movement was largely limited to the latter, for it lacked any definite economic program. The British Chartists included many workers, increasing numbers of whom were in distress from the prolonged industrial depression of the late 1830s, which extended into the following decade.

The People's Charter was drawn up in 1838 and presented to Parliament for acceptance in early 1839. It called for (1) the granting of the franchise to every male person over twenty-one years of age; (2) voting by ballot; (3) annual parliaments; (4) equal electoral districts; (5) no property qualifications for members of Parliament; and (6) payment of members of Parliament. The charter was rejected—and in a manner that showed that Parliament had no intention of considering it seriously.

During 1839 there were riots and much political agitation by the Chartists, which culminated in the arrests of most of the leaders by the end of the year. Nevertheless, under the leadership of Feargus O'Connor (1794–1855), a second Chartist petition was presented to Parliament in 1842, and it, too, was overwhelmingly rejected. A final attempt was made in 1848, but after it too fizzled the Chartist movement quickly disappeared.

Instead of setting out to reform only the political arm of the capitalist state, other movements attempted to reform and use its economic services as well to benefit the working classes. This was true of Louis Blanc, the French socialist politician and journalist, whom we met in Chapter 2 and who proposed national workshops for the purpose. It was also true of Ferdinand Lassalle, the German socialist and lawyer, who wanted the state to finance producer cooperatives that would be established by the working classes.

It was Ferdinand Lassalle (1825–1864), not Karl Marx, who supplied the chief impetus for the formation of the General German Workers' Association in 1863, which was the first workers' political party in Germany, and which later, in 1875, developed into the Social Democratic party. It was the program of this party, heavily infused with Lassallian doctrine, that Marx attacked so severely in his Critique of the Gotha Programme.

Lassalle, in a very general way, accepted Marx's analysis of the exploitation of labor by capital, although he ascribed much of the exploitation to the ability of capitalists to capture the extra product coming from the division of labor. Moreover, he appended to Marx's analysis an "iron law of wages" (the phrase being his invention) which, he argued, held workers to minimal living standards. The only way to circumvent this law was to transform industry by the formation of producers' associations, with ownership and control in the hands of the workers. In this way, the distinction between profits and wages would disappear, and so would the iron law. Lassalle believed that this industrial transformation would have to be accomplished by the state, which he saw as an engine for the regeneration of mankind. At least it was potentially such an engine, for the state would reach this exalted status only after it came to represent all the people. Consequently, the immediate task was to organize the workers into a political party for the purpose of fighting for universal suffrage.

Lassalle, then, had a theory of the state that was decidedly at odds with Marx's. In the latter's view, the state was the agent of the capitalist class, and only when the working classes overthrew it and captured political power themselves would they be able to solve their most basic problems. But for Lassalle, the state was almost divine, capable of bringing about the transformation of all of society in the interests of the masses. Marx understandably scorned what he considered to be this foolish fancy. But that fancy captured the allegiance of large numbers of workers, and it was substantially more influential in these ranks than revolutionary Marxism for many years.

Lassalle's life was cut short by death in a duel over a love affair.

Anarchism, Syndicalism, and Guild Socialism

Anarchism. Anarchism, syndicalism, and guild socialism were movements dedicated to the destruction of the political state as soon as possible and once and for all. Anarchism appeared first. It was a protest, primarily by the petty bourgeoisie, craftsmen, and peasants, against the forces of capitalism that were uprooting them, centralizing and bureaucratizing more and more areas of political and economic life, and increasing the dependency of each person on all others through the increasing division of labor brought about by the Industrial Revolution. Anarchism was a doctrine that individual liberty can be attained only by eliminating all authority and laws, and substituting for them (1) mutual agreements among the members of society and (2) the sum of social customs and habits. The principal authority to be eliminated was the state. The doctrine was based on the beliefs that artificial institutions corrupt what would otherwise be a natural and good society and that the highest aim for man is individual liberty.

This movement was strongest in regions and countries that were poorest and least developed industrially. With a few exceptions, it was weakest in areas possessing strong urban working classes. Thus, anarchism found its most fertile soil in the Latin countries—where capitalism had taken hold but was developing more slowly. The movement, nevertheless, attracted a following almost everywhere.

The inroads that anarchism and related doctrines made on revolutionary Marxism are well exemplified by the movement associated with the ideas of Pierre-Joseph Proudhon, the French social theorist. His ideas had much more currency among European workers than Marx's for several decades, including the crucial ones of the 1840s through the 1870s. Many workers were opposed to Marx's authoritarian and centralist notions and to his proposals for nationalization of the means of production. They had greater regard for Proudhon's more libertarian views, his emphasis on the autonomy of smaller groups, and his "practical" schemes for cheap credit and fair exchanges of workers' products—ways of beating capitalism by peacefully constructing alternative economic institutions around it rather than by Marx's way of a head-on bloody political revolt against it.

Proudhon (1809–1865) sought justice, which he thought of as equality and as freedom of the individual from constraints. In the name of individual freedom, he therefore opposed both church and state. And, in the interest of equality, he opposed the exploitation of workers by employers (who failed to pay workers for the extra productivity that arose from the collective force of workers) and by middlemen and financiers. His was a world of villages, small industries, the family, and the individual; at the level of the nation, a world of federations—or, better, simply groupings of families. He spoke on behalf of the petty bourgeoisie, the family, and craftspeople, and against big financial and industrial wealth.

During his lifetime, Proudhon's influence was primarily in France, but also, less strongly, in the French-speaking parts of Belgium and Switzerland. However, in the middle 1860s, it began to spread to other parts of Switzerland, Italy, and Spain. His views proved particularly potent among French trade unionists and socialists. During the 1860s, the majority of French socialists were Proudhonists who were hostile to Marx's collectivism. When trade unions were fully legalized in 1884, the workers who followed Proudhon were in the vanguard in establishing the unions. By the early years of this century, Proudhonism was the leading force in the French trade unions and succeeded in separating them from political movements in that country—that is, in confining them to economic programs. Moreover, the 1871 Paris Commune, formed by the workers of that city in opposition to the national government at the conclusion of the Franco-Prussian War, was led, not by Marxists, but by the followers of Proudhon, as well as by those of Louis-Auguste Blanqui, the French revolutionist.

Blanqui (1805–1881) was a radical thinker and a man of action who espoused insurrection by a small group of revolutionists. He spent about 60 percent of his adult life in prisons for acting on such beliefs. Blanqui believed that workers were exploited under capitalism, primarily by being overcharged as consumers rather than, as Marx taught, by being underpaid as producers. He proposed to overthrow capitalism with a small disciplined group, in a seizure of power by a coup d'etat, after which a dictatorship would be established for the purpose of guiding the education of the people in republican ideas (and against the church) so that eventually they could be prepared for the new society of communism. He thought of this new society as a cooperative one, in which self-governing industrial and agricultural associations would replace the state. Blanqui differed from Marx not only in his weaker analysis of capitalism, as illustrated by his theory of exploitation, but also in his shunning of mass working-class movements in favor of secret insurrectionary armies and in his notions of socialism as decentralized economic associations.

Proudhonists for a time dominated the International Workingmen's Association, which Karl Marx had helped to form in 1864. In the end, it was

French socialist Pierre-Joseph Proudhon axing down the ramparts of capitalism. (The Bettmann Archive, Inc.)

the powerful challenge from Michael Bakunin, Proudhon's disciple, that convinced Marx to transfer the headquarters of the International to America so as to remove it from Bakunin's influence.

Bakunin (1814–1876) was a Russian revolutionist and perhaps the most celebrated advocate of anarchism in the world. He opposed the privileged classes, supported the working classes, denounced bourgeois society and its universal exploitative tendencies, but thought that the most pernicious evil was not exploitation but tyranny. Thus, he primarily opposed anything that infringed on individual liberty. He repudiated all authority, especially that of God and the state. To Bakunin every state supported the privileged few against the poor majority, and every church was an ally of the state in this and other forms of subjugation. Although Bakunin opposed all government, he saw "society" as natural and good: It does not limit people's liberty, but, on the contrary, it is only within society that they can find their liberty. He endorsed the revolutionary destruction of everything oppressive, of "civilization." He believed that revolution would come either by a peasant uprising or by a spontaneous revolt of a town mob, but in either case would be quite unorganized.

Thus, contrary to Marx, Bakunin relied as much on the peasantry as on the urban working class for the revolution, indeed on all of the downtrodden masses. Moreover, he rejected political action to achieve revolution—that is, he rejected the taking of political power by the revolutionists. Instead, the revolution had to be social—revolutionizing society by abolishing the state. Nevertheless, he sought the establishment of a select and tightly organized revolutionary party, which was contradictory to his other views. Bakunin, like Marx, thought of revolution in Hegelian dialectical terms, but, unlike Marx, he saw it mostly in idealist form, as the "free, inevitable development of a free spirit." Revolution, he said, was more instinct than thought. He refused to acknowledge any laws of history or any ready-made system to save the world. He warned against such system makers (i.e., Marx) and the possible rule of intellectuals.

Although Marxists did not expect the communist movement to make great progress in the more backward areas of Europe (in Spain and Italy, in particular), whatever progress it might have made was diminished and postponed by anarchism's—and later syndicalism's—greater attraction. The Spanish and Italian sections of the International, for example, were devoted to Bakunin, and it was he who was instrumental in igniting the vigorous anarchist movement in Italy during the 1870s. After that, Italian anarchism dwindled, as the more radical workers turned to parliamentary socialism and some of the key figures became infatuated with utopian communities—another instance of the persistence of the utopian dream, which itself continued to weaken the Marxist movements. After the turn of the century when the revolutionary fervor revived, the outlet for it was syndicalism and not revolutionary Marxism. Marxism came to Italy in force only on the shoulders of Lenin after the October Revolution in 1917, but before long its aspect, too, became reformism, under the leadership of

Palmiro Togliatti (1893–1964), who followed a more liberal and nationalistic line than was desired by the Soviets.

Proudhon's notions infiltrated into Spain as early as the 1840s. They became important in the next two decades, and by 1870 his main works were widely available in Spanish. By this time, however, Bakunin's more radical version of anarchism had made its appearance, and after that Kropotkin's views made a significant impact in workers' circles.

Prince Piotr Kropotkin (1842–1921), a Russian, was Bakunin's outstanding disciple. However, Kropotkin did not accept the concept of a conspiratorial revolutionary party that would carry out a coup d'etat, favoring instead a more spontaneous uprising of the masses. But he agreed with Bakunin that the revolution should be social, not political. Although he accepted the highly decentralized federation of associations, he believed that workers should receive payment according to their needs and not, as Bakunin wanted, according to their performances or productivity. Kropotkin regarded output as the collective work of humanity, of present and past generations. No worker's output, therefore, could be identified as his alone.

He also rejected the thesis that the competitive struggle dominated the evolution of biological species. Of greater importance, he felt, was the cooperative spirit—mutual aid. In his good society, people would work in small groups, and the associated technology would allow each worker to engage his talents in a variety of ways: mental and manual labor and agricultural and industrial work would be combined. (These elements of Kropotkin's good society, which can be traced far back into Marxist and radical thought, have turned up time and time again in communist literature. Mao Zedong, for example, relying on his own background, voiced them repeatedly as desirable goals for Chinese society.)

The Spanish Federation of the International Workingmen's Association, an anarchist federation that Marx attempted to wean away from Bakunin but could not, was formed in 1870; this organization, in a move contrary to orthodox Marxism, was expanded to include peasants and landless laborers. Anarchism, in various forms, remained the dominant revolutionary expression in Spain through the rest of the century and into the present one, until syndicalism successfully vied with it. Revolutionary Marxism was seldom a serious contender during these years. In 1910 the Confederacion Nacional del Trabajo was formed mainly of worker-anarchists, who remained in control of the organization thereafter. Its membership grew to seven hundred thousand by 1919, to one-and-a-half million by the mid-1930s. However, by the end of the Spanish civil war, anarchism in Spain was definitely on the decline, which eventually provided some room for Marxists.

The anarchists often saw the same evils of society that Marx did. Instead of identifying the source of these evils within the capitalist mode of production, Bakunin and the other anarchists believed that the font was the state, which for Marx was simply the executive committee of the bourgeoisie. Further, for Marx, the state, as the dictatorship of the proletariat, was required after the revolution. The anarchists wished its elimination immediately. Marx visualized the state fading away as a class institution only after the socialist period led into the classless society of communism.

Syndicalism. Syndicalism was a doctrine, and the movement based on it, that revolutionary trade unionism, and not political-parliamentary action, would achieve the victory of the workers over capitalists, a victory that would result in the replacement of the state and its machinery by a congress of trade unions, and in the replacement of political democracy by economic or working-class democracy. Syndicalism flourished from the 1890s through the 1920s, during which time it attracted many workers away from Marxism and political action generally. Syndicalism was a protest against the ineffective political action of reformist Marxists, who advocated working through democratic institutions toward their goals. It was also a protest against the peaceful paths of other erstwhile revolutionists and a response to the failures of anarchism. Syndicalism was originally a French movement of the 1890s, which later spread to Italy, the United States (as the Industrial Workers of the World), and a few other countries.

While socialists in the United States were trying to influence the more conservative trade unions, many were also operating at the other end of the spectrum, in the International Workers of the World (IWW, or Wobblies), which came together in 1905 and saw its demise in the early 1920s. A few years after its establishment, the IWW began concentrating on those workers neglected by the mainstream of the labor movement. It had immediate aims of improving the lives of these workers, but it also sought, in the long run, the revolutionary overthrow of capitalism. "Arise, ye prisoners of starvation! Arise, ye wretched of the earth! For Justice thunders condemnation. A better world's in birth." Thus began the IWW's song about the coming revolution.

The rank and file disdained political parties and politics in general; they considered themselves economic activists, not political intellectuals. The IWW insisted that political power was only a reflection of economic power, and so it was the latter that it sought— by direct action: conventional and wildcat strikes, passive resistance, sabotage, and, at the supreme moment, the general strike. All of these actions, rather than parliamentary politics or socialist wrangling, would gain higher wages and shorter hours and, in the end, the downfall of the wage system—if the working class could be organized into "one big union."

After the toppling of capitalism, the state would disappear, worker-organized industries taking its place. Thus the IWW had syndicalist aims and tactics touched with the anarchist's brush. Its efforts reflected similar movements going on in Europe at about the same time. It was, however, as much the left wing of the labor movement as it was a socialist movement. In the end, the Wobblies were weakened by their own contradictory goals (unionism and revolution) and then repressed by the government—through raids, arrests, deportations—shortly after the First World War.

Syndicalists, like anarchists, wished to destroy the state as an instrument of oppression. They viewed trade unions not only as the basic unit of production but as the basic unit of all society. Trade unions were to equip the workers educationally and morally for their future leadership roles. To achieve their aims, the syndicalists advocated direct industrial action, such as the general strike. Although syndicalists held to the core of revolutionary Marxism—the class struggle—they departed from those precepts in eschewing political action, in striving not to transcend bourgeois democracy but to establish industrial democracy.

The tactic of the general strike, by stopping all work, was meant to energize the proletariat, sharpen class divisions, and invigorate class warfare—and ultimately, of course, to be the vehicle for the overthrow of the capitalist system. For Georges Sorel (1847–1922), the French social philosopher whose book, *Reflections on Violence* (1908), was one of the bibles of the movement, the general strike was the necessary social myth, a socialist equivalent of Christianity's Second Coming, that would move the workers to action. Aside from strikes, syndicalists proposed that class warfare could be carried out by sabotage and by antipatriotic and antimilitaristic campaigns.

Guild Socialism. Guild socialism was the British version of syndicalism, which, however, went beyond the Continental movement by combining collectivism (Marxism) with syndicalism. It got under way during the 1910s, faded out in the 1920s, and died in the 1930s. According to this assembly of radicals, the guilds would represent the workers, whereas the state, greatly attenuated, would represent consumers. Guild socialism emphasized the organization of the work place and its control by workers; it set out to destroy the wage system and the conditions that made labor a commodity for sale. Production would be for use and not for profit.

One strand of this movement led back to the Middle Ages and the guilds of that time, investing them with the qualities missing from the industrial work places of the day: production for use, the pride of high-quality workmanship, only slight differences between employers and employees. The structure of present-day trade unions had to be brought into line not only with the high principles of medieval times but with the modern trends in industry.

Guild socialists rejected both parliament and the state as useful centers around which to build the new society, and hence they disdained a legislated welfare socialism and a state socialism of nationalized industries. Their doctrine was that parliament is based on universal representation, which amounts to no representation at all, for a true democracy is a functional one—that is, based on groups of people each having a common functional relation to economic society. In the new society, a Central Guild Congress, comprising the functional guilds, would look after the interests of the workers, while a truncated state and parliament would own the means of production and function in the consumer area.

Guild socialism employed important elements of Marxism in its theory, but it departed from Marxism in its proposal for a weak socialist state, in its syndicalist features, in its romantic notions of the past, and in some of the moderate tactics it advocated for achieving its aims. For a time, it aided in deflecting workers away from Marxism and in obfuscating Marxist notions of appropriate actions for the solution of workers' grievances.

Marxists as Reformers

In many countries, revolutionary Marxism faced dissolution from within—from its members who wanted to reform capitalism by stages until it would be transformed into a socialist society, a goal that they hoped to attain by working through capitalism's democratic institutions. Such Marxists have been called "revisionists" by their more revolutionary comrades.

German Social Democracy. In Germany, reformist elements rose to the top almost immediately. In fact, Marxism in Germany was probably reformist from its very beginning, with Marxist deputies satisfied with being elected to a powerless Reichstag. German Marxism, or Social Democracy, was led by Wilhelm Liebknecht (1826–1900) and his disciple August Bebel (1840–1913), both of whom were more democratic radicals than revolutionary Marxists. In 1869, Liebknecht and Bebel formed the Social Democratic Labor party, which in 1875, at Gotha, merged with Ferdinand Lassalle's group, the General German Workers' Association, to form the Socialist Labor party, later known as the Social Democratic party of Germany (S.P.D.). It is this party, long shorn of its revolutionary aims, that came to power in 1969 under Willy Brandt, who was followed by Helmut Schmidt.

Prior to its formation, this new party issued its famous Gotha Programme, which Marx vitriolized as being theoretically inadequate, historically blind, strategically naive, and full of the theoretical errors of Lassalle. Marx concluded his critique with: "I have spoken and saved my soul." But, according to the Marxian scholar John Lewis, in *The Life and Teaching of Karl Marx*, Marx's censure "made no impression on the leaders of the new party. Even those who professed to be Marxist shared in the prevailing theoretical confusion." Much of the party, not knowing what to make of Marx (few of the members had ever read his *Das Kapital*), turned to the more appealing works of Eugen Karl Dühring (1833–1921), who wanted to retain capitalism while eliminating its abuses through a strong labor movement.

The reformist character of German Social Democracy was revealed in its policy statement of 1879, issued from Switzerland, where some of the leaders fled as a result of Bismarck's Exclusion Bill of 1878, which limited the freedom of socialists. This document was also attacked by Marx and

Engels in a letter sent to its principal authors in September of that year. In their letter, Marx and Engels accused the Social Democratic party of wanting to be "all-sided" instead of proletarian; of wanting to win over the bourgeoisie, in the belief that the workers are incapable of emancipating themselves; of advocating "legality" and "reform" and shunning revolution. They also attacked the party for advocating "all sorts of petty rubbish and the patching up of the capitalist order of society in order at least to produce the appearance of something happening without at the same time scaring the bourgeoisie."

The party leaders presented, Marx and Engels complained, a petty bourgeois program, "full of anxiety that the proletariat, under the pressure of its revolutionary position, may 'go too far.' " This program, they accused, devoted "its whole strength and energy to those petty-bourgeois patchwork reforms which, by providing the old order of society with new props, may perhaps transform the ultimate catastrophe into a gradual, piecemeal, and as far as possible peaceful process of dissolution." Marx and Engels concluded by noting that the policy statement implied that the workers are too uneducated to emancipate themselves and must first be freed from above by philanthropic capitalists. In this letter, the authors were distressed at how little progress in the understanding of Marxism had been made since the *Communist Manifesto* was published in 1848—that is, in the course of thirty years!

The antisocialist legislation was lifted in 1890, and the Social Democrats held their first legal congress in Germany in 1891. On its surface, the Erfurt Programme that resulted was a revolutionary Marxist document. However, there was a world of difference between the programme's revolutionary theoretical statements and its reformist practical demands. So far as the theoretical statements were concerned, the orthodox and the revisionist Marxist wings of the party were far apart. But when it came right down to actual programs, the similarities between the two were the more striking. Karl Kautsky (1854–1938), who was the principal author of the Erfurt Programme, taught the party to rely on the relentless march of history for the final overthrow of capitalism, while he continued to interpret Marx in activist revolutionary terms. In effect, his iron outlook of economic determinism disarmed the party by persuading its members that revolutionary action was unnecessary so long as history was there to do the job. This further reinforced the party's bourgeois democratic, reformist tendencies.

These tendencies were given an additional boost by the work of Eduard Bernstein, a German socialist and a prominent member of the Social Democratic party. As a result of Bismarck's antisocialist legislation in 1878, Bernstein left Germany for Switzerland and then England, not returning to his native land for over twenty years. In England, he was greatly influenced by the Fabians and other social reformist movements, to the extent that he eventually came out openly against Marx's theories of class struggles, proletarian revolutions, and much else. His "revisionist" views were contained in his principal work, *Evolutionary Socialism* (1899). After his return to Berlin in 1901, he became the leader of the revisionist faction of the Social Democratic party, his main opponent being Kautsky, the latter who, at least in words, upheld the more revolutionary side of Marxism. Still, the two of them, taken together, greatly weakened revolutionary Marxism as an activist prescription.

Eduard Bernstein (1850–1932) claimed that economic, social, and political conditions had changed greatly since Marx surveyed the scene, with the result that many of Marx's analyses and predictions were badly outdated. Compared to Marx's day, the situation of the 1890s in Western Europe had changed markedly: Workers' living standards were substantially higher, democracy and universal suffrage were spreading, reforms were more likely than ever to favor the working classes, and trade union activity was quite encouraging—so wrote Bernstein.

Bernstein went on to argue that capitalism was showing an increasing capacity to adapt to new conditions, to remedy its excesses, and to control itself. This was reflected, first, in crises becoming less severe, owing to the development of the credit system, which corrected financial imbalances rapidly; to the growth of employers' organizations, which allowed for greater planning; and to the widening of the means of communication, which permitted the rapid dissemination of information. Capitalism's new orderliness was reflected, second, in the rise of the middle classes, which itself was brought about by the growing differentiation of the branches of production and the increasing number of skilled and technical jobs created by the continuing growth of the productive forces. Capitalism's adaptability was reflected, third, in the amelioration of the economic and political condition of the proletariat, which stemmed largely from their increasingly successful trade union activity.

Therefore, Bernstein contended that a socialist party enrolling a major section of the electorate and linked with trade unions and cooperatives could achieve socialism within a democratically constituted polity by use of constitutional means—that is, without revolution. He emphasized that he favored socialism over capitalism, but he urged his followers to forget ultimate aims and to work on the means, making these the goals.

Bernstein's effectiveness within the Marxist movements in Western Europe lay not only in the fact that many conditions had changed since Marx wrote but also in his use (though superficial) of Marxian analysis to refute Marx himself.

British Reformists and Fabians. Revolutionary Marxism was in equal trouble almost everywhere else. In Great Britain, for example, Marx and Engels repeatedly noted, from the late 1850s on, that the British workers lacked revolutionary motivation. They attributed this to various factors, including the emigration of the most advanced workers to America and Australia, the workers' nationalistic response to British imperialism, the pacification of workers with temporarily higher wages, the splitting of the proletariat into the hostile camps of English and Irish workers, the contentment of the workers owing to prolonged prosperity, and the presence of corrupt trade union leaders.

The first Marxist party in Britain was formed by H.M. Hyndman (1842–1921), an English journalist and socialist. In 1881 he founded the Social Democratic Federation, which became the Social Democratic party in 1908, and in 1911 merged with the other left-wing socialist groups to form the British Socialist party. But Hyndman's understanding of Marxism was quite deficient, and Marx, in his last years, did not regard the party as a real proletarian movement; it was laced with reformist webs.

The Fabian socialists were a more thoroughly reformist group in Britain. This socialist society was organized in 1884 by Frank Podmore and Edward Pease and was soon joined by George Bernard Shaw (1856–1950) and Sidney Webb (1859–1947), its two leading proponents. The society opposed revolutionary Marxism, holding that socialism could be achieved through social reforms and the socialistic "permeation" of existing political institutions. The Fabians considered the march to socialism to be a gradual, continuing process that evolved from individualism to collectivism, an almost-inevitable historical movement. The existing political institutions were, therefore, useful in enabling the present society to be transformed into a socialist one. The Fabians were more interpreters of this ongoing historical process than activists within it. As such, they, too, served to turn workers and intellectuals away from revolutionary Marxism.

The Fabians rejected Marx's labor theory of value and its associated analyses of surplus value and exploitation of labor. However, they held to the belief that labor was exploited by capital, backing this up theoretically by looking to Henry George (1839–1897, American economist and social reformer), whose analysis turned on the unearned incomes of land rent. The Fabians extended this concept to include all "surplus incomes." These incomes arise, they thought, from the fact that identical commodities are often produced at different costs and yet sell at the same price; those produced under the most favorable circumstances, therefore, yield a surplus to their producers. The Fabians proposed that the state appropriate, by taxation, nationalization, or other means, these surpluses, and use them for the public good.

The Fabians relished the values of efficiency, collective endeavors, state bureaucratic direction, expertise of administrators and technicians—often at some expense to individualism, democratic processes, and class struggle. "They were more grieved by the world's mess," wrote the economic historian Alexander Gray, in The Socialist Tradition, *"than hurt by the world's wrongs." They were among the first to work, even if unknowingly, for the modern mixed economy and the welfare state.*

The Fabians later helped to establish the unified Labour Representation Committee, which evolved into the British Labour party.

Marxism's Competitors and Their Capitalist Origins

Each of the dissident movements we have examined emanated from capitalism's own development. Because this development had an orderly advance, the dissident movements themselves followed one another in a logical sequence. Utopian socialists, for example, reacted impractically against the ills of early industrial capitalism because of insufficient insight in that early period about capitalism's future path. A short time later, Chartism was based on the growing economic freedoms enjoyed by workers and others in the commercial and in the financial arenas, and their attempt to capture similar gains within the area of political democracy.

Later radicals focused on the growing power of the state, which preceded the development of a mature urban working class, as the font of society's ills. The anarchists proposed to smash the state. When, later, the urban workers became numerous and better organized, radical leaders undertook to use the state or to reform it to benefit the workers. Revolutionary Marxism envisaged the urban workers as ultimately carrying out a revolution against the capitalist class. Hence, this radical movement did not appear until the emergence of the urban proletariat. However, because further capitalist development improved the lives of many workers, gave them space to organize, and opened political processes to them, Marxism became less revolutionary and more reformist.

Syndicalism appeared later because it had to await the fuller development of trade unions and the failure of reformist Marxism to make progress through the political institutions of capitalism. Guild socialism followed, for it was an amalgam of the syndicalists' reliance on trade unions and the Marxists' collectivist tendencies.

Thus, each stage of capitalist development produced certain assaults against capitalism. As time passed, a plethora of such anticapitalist movements accumulated—promoted, too, by splits within each movement. Each battalion existed side by side and struggled against the others, making it unlikely that any one of them could succeed in its aim of overcoming the contemporary society. The array of anticapitalist movements rendered revolutionary Marxism more or less impotent for many decades. In the end, Marxism had to jump hedges, from the advanced to the more backward areas of capitalism, before it could find fertile ground for revolution.

The Failure of Socialism and Communism in the United States

Although socialism and communism (Marxism) have at times shown some marginal strength in the United States, these movements on the whole have been weak, and it is clear that they have not even come close to capturing political power. On a few occasions in presidential elections, the Socialist party approached a million votes, the Communist party a hundred thousand, and the Socialist Labor party (followers of Leon Trotsky) fifty thousand, but on a national basis these are insignificant totals. Although socialists have done somewhat better at the local levels, even there such successes were concentrated in the first few decades of this century and are now only memories of the distant past. What accounts for socialism's failure to make more headway?

Absence of a Feudal Past

Some scholars have argued that socialism has been feeble because of the absence of a "feudal experience" in the United States. Louis Hartz, the Harvard political scientist, takes this to mean three things. First, the absence of a feudal past signifies that there was no aristocratic culture to communicate a sense of class to the capitalists (the bourgeoisie), and no aristocracy and class-conscious bourgeoisie to pass on the class heritage to the workers. Second, the absence of a feudal past means that the capitalists did not have to carry out a social revolution against a ruling class, and hence the working classes failed to inherit a revolutionary tradition. Third, the absence of a feudal past means there was no memory of the medieval corporate spirit which the working classes could attempt to recreate, in reaction to liberalism, by some form of modern collectivism. This argument, then, insists that a robust working-class movement along socialist lines requires a feudal past to bequeath it an understanding of class, of social revolution, and of the possibilities of collective life. If the workers and the country lack these legacies, socialism quickly degenerates into individualism and reformism.

According to this line of argument, when the great migration that created America left behind in the Old World the experiences of class, revolution, and collectiveness, it left behind as well the seeds of European socialism. In short, a nation that has skipped feudalism and hence the revolution against feudalism is not likely to find socialism. It is more likely to try to improve the capitalism it has.

However, inasmuch as revolutionary Marxism failed in all of the advanced capitalist countries, in many with a strong feudal past and in a few without such a past, other factors must have been involved in these failures. Nevertheless, although failing to capture political power, revolutionary Marxism and socialism in general have been more potent in Great Britain and in Western Europe than in the United States, a fact which suggests that in these terms socialist strength may indeed be linked to a country's progression from feudalism to capitalism. In a sense, America was born modern and so lacked the necessary background for acute class struggles.

Immigration, Land, and Wealth

Socialism in the United States has been weakened, too, by the successive waves of immigration that created ethnic, racial, and religious cleavages within the working classes and so prevented any united action against the capitalist system. This factor can be coupled with the open frontiers of America, which provided an escape from dissatisfactions, unemployment, and dead-end situations. The success of capitalism, within an environment of rich untapped natural resources, in raising standards of living of the masses was also an important factor in dampening radical propensities.

The knife of immigration, however, cuts both ways. In one direction, it was the immigrants in the latter half of the nineteenth century, especially the German immigrants, who brought socialist ideas and practices with them to America. Moreover, discrimination against newly arrived immigrants turned some of them toward the leftist movements. It took some time for socialism to establish itself as a "native product." In the other direction, the ethnic, racial, and religious diversities among immigrants reduced opportunities for political solidarity of the working classes by continuing to splinter them in many different ways. On balance, large-scale immigration was an important vehicle for the diffusion of socialist notions in the New World, but the diffusion took place within an increasingly fractured working class that was unable or uninterested, as a class-conscious body, to act on them.

Proletarian solidarity was also ruptured by the opportunities available to many workers, who would otherwise have been trapped, to move westward. Furthermore, the vast spaces themselves served to make communication among elements of the working classes and concerted action extremely difficult. The presence of the frontier reduced the Marxian "reserve army of labor" (the army of unemployed) and probably, thereby, kept wages higher than they otherwise would have been.

Given this open land—much of it conquered from Native Americans and Mexicans—and the wealth of natural resources, the system of capitalism provided rising standards of living for many workers. The periods of prosperity clearly outweighed the years of economic doldrums. The long-term production gains that the new continent allowed were translated into higher wages for American workers than those received in the Old World. This in itself tended to reduce any ill will toward existing institutions that otherwise might have built up, therefore making it less likely that workers would seek political movements aimed at overthrowing those institutions.

Americanism as Substitute Socialism

The weakness of socialism and communism in the United States can also be ascribed to the presence of American values that could be substituted for those of socialism—and, hence, to the preemption by "Americanism" as the ideology of the working classes. Accordingly, some scholars have argued that the set of beliefs that comprises Americanism—including beliefs in equality of opportunity, of upward social mobility, of higher rewards for greater individual effort—has satisfied most workers, making it less likely that they would search around for others. It is this ideology that contributed to bread-and-butter unionism, which induced many workers to aim for more money rather than the social reconstruction of America. It is this ideology that supported the somewhat anarchistic bent, the extreme individualism, of the American. As the labor leader Gus Tyler has put it, in an essay in *Failure of a Dream?* (edited by J.H.M. Laslett and S.M. Lipset): "The continent was peopled by runaways from authority." And such runaways were looking for liberty, not socialist collectivism.

Internal Weaknesses of Socialist Movements

Taking a different tack, it can be argued that the source of socialism's weakness lies within socialism itself. Its constant factionalism, its inability to reconcile its ethics with the demands of political expediency, its mistaken analyses of American society or of the direction of its movement, and the inability of the middle-class socialist intellectuals to comprehend the aims and aspirations of the working classes—all of these and more can be specified. One can also blame the conservative bent of labor unions, which might have been more closely associated with the socialist parties.

It is certainly true that socialist parties in America, like those almost everywhere else, have often fought each other more furiously than they have the capitalist class. Why do radical movements, such as these, have so strong a tendency to split and disintegrate?

Personal animosities and personal ambitions for power have sometimes led to these internecine battles, as they have in politics generally, whatever the ideological persuasion. Then, too, many of these radical movements were based on the theory and practice of Marxism, and on the writings of Marx and Engels themselves. Because of the intricacy of Marxist theory, various interpretations arose of it and different conclusions were drawn about tactics employed by socialist parties in pursuit of what they understood to be Marxist aims. People of principle stood up for what they believed to be correct, and, if a certain religious fervor was sometimes used as a topping, the sacred ground could be defended unto the last. Some leaders and their followers refused to make any compromise or to accept any impurity into their ranks.

Another reason for the factionalism and splits within socialist movements in America was the continuing strength of the adversary—capitalism—and the psychological pressures exerted thereby on all of these dissident groups. Although expectations often ran high, political defeats were constant and crushing, and bitter debates and criminations almost always followed. Many dedicated socialists found it increasingly difficult to make a living and thus to support their families, either because they gave their time too generously to the party or because ordinary livelihoods were closed to them. Spies and provocateurs within the movement were always a threat, and their disclosure often caused painful readjustments. Under these conditions, socialist leaders and their followers sometimes displayed the strain that they were under, manifested in fissures within what might otherwise have been a more unified effort.

The very process through which capitalism developed in the United States created conditions for splits within the ranks of the enemies of that system. Although most socialists, and presumably all communists, represent in some general sense "the proletariat," as capitalist economic development takes place the composition of that class changes. As a consequence, some factions within a party are favored and others disfavored, changing the balance of power within the party. Economic development, for example, may reduce the rural and increase the urban working class, or enhance the weight of westerners as opposed to easterners, or of debtors over creditors. Because these class and group formations within the economy are represented within socialist and communist parties, any substantial changes in such formations will create internal party tensions.

Moreover, much the same thing happens owing to capitalism's strong propensity (necessity, many Marxists would claim) to develop cyclically— that is, with ups and downs, prosperities followed by recessions or depressions. These capitalist cycles are transmitted, inversely, to capitalism's socialist and communist adversaries, for these radical movements tend to prosper when capitalism is depressed and to languish when capitalism is buoyant. Such cycles within dissident movements create severe strains between those members who are basically reformers and those who are basically revolutionists. During capitalist downturns, when the dissidents are gaining strength, the revolutionists have the upper hand. In the opposite situation, the reformers take over. These shifting fortunes are sometimes enough to wreck the unity of a movement or party. Thus, when one considers both the secular and the cyclical development of capitalism, and also takes account of the basic long-run strength of the capitalist mode of production in the United States, the stresses and strains generated within radical movements become apparent.

The Proliferation of Socialist Movements

We have seen previously that European capitalism created not only its chief antagonist, Marxism, but also Marxism's competitors, and by so doing neutralized the chief revolutionary threats against capitalism itself. Much the same thing occurred in the United States, with Marxist parties competing against syndicalist movements, revolutionists against reformers, those championing rural demands opposed to those lobbying for urban needs, labor organizers vying with currency reformers, anarchists with collectivists, and so on. In fact, the profusion of radical movements in the United States largely reflected Europe's own anticapitalist formations and their sources. Hence, in its general outlines, most of the previous analysis in this chapter applies to the United States as well as to Europe. In America, too, the particular way in which capitalism developed generated a lavish variety of anticapitalist movements, each competing against the others in such a way as to weaken them all.

Repression

Another reason for the weakness of socialism and communism in the United States is that, whenever they have threatened the existing order, they have been repressed by the government. In the aftermath of the Haymarket Square riot in Chicago in 1886, eight anarchists were convicted of a murder for which no evidence connecting them with the crime was produced. Several thousand radicals were prosecuted under the Espionage Act of 1917 and the Sedition Act of 1918. Many leaders and members of the radical Industrial Workers of the World were thrown in jail during and after the First World War for sabotage, draft evasion, crippling essential war industries, and other crimes. Also, after that war, the Palmer raids incarcerated thousands of "subversive" aliens, and some were deported. After the Second World War, there were further repressive laws, the McCarthy attacks, drives against the Black Panthers, and the illegal infiltration of radical movements by the FBI and the CIA. The two world wars, in view of the traditional pacifism of much of the socialist movement, turned many people against socialism; and the wars also presented the government with an excuse to crack down on these dissidents, many of whom served prison terms for their objections to the fighting.

Financial Sirens

Industrial capitalism created not only rivals to revolutionary Marxism but also a variety of financial problems that captured the attention of the working classes. Workers on both sides of the Atlantic, but especially in the United States, channeled much of their energies into trying to find solutions to these financial disorders, much to the detriment of Marxism, other socialist movements, and even trade unions.

Economic systems generally comprise three areas of activity: (1) producing, (2) buying and selling, and (3) lending and borrowing. As capitalism develops, the second and third areas for some time grow very rapidly relative to the first. Buying and selling proliferate because production becomes increasingly specialized, necessitating trades among the special-

Haymarket Square "anarchists" hanged on circumstantial evidence. (The Bettmann Archive, Inc.)

ists; and people become decreasingly self-sufficient, as they leave farming and other self-employment and take up work for others. Lending and borrowing gain enormously owing to the growth of specialization between savers and investors—that is, those who save loan money to those who invest—and among financial institutions and financial markets. Commercial activity and financial transactions, therefore, soar relative to the economy's production of goods and services. Moreover, at the same time, capitalist development generates business cycles. During economic downturns, there are often banking collapses, currency disorders, and market disruptions; during upturns, financial speculations and stock market booms are frequently featured.

Many people, therefore, become increasingly involved in buying and selling and in lending and borrowing as capitalism advances, and so they become more aware of periodic malfunctioning in these two areas. They are more and more inclined to attribute their poverty, loss of jobs, and other economic ills to such currency and commercial disorders. Since the Marxist conviction is that workers suffer because, not owning the means of production, they can be exploited at work, and that such exploitation is enhanced when some are unemployed, a conflict develops between the Marxist perception of reality and the way increasing numbers of workers come to view the economic system.

Accordingly, during much of the nineteenth century in the United States, workers and farmers devoted substantial portions of their time and energy to currency and banking problems, the solutions to which mattered little to their positions subordinate to the capital-owning class. These issues concerned the role of a central bank in the life of a nation, the disposition of the greenbacks (inconvertible paper money) issued during the Civil War, and the place of gold and silver in the monetary system. President Jackson's long and bitter campaign against the Second Bank of the United States, the spirited political debates and new parties formed during President Grant's tenure around the issue of whether to increase or decrease the greenbacks, and William Jennings Bryan's crusade in the 1890s for free and unlimited coinage of silver, culminating in his famous "Cross of Gold" speech in 1896—each of these issues brought the working classes to fever pitch, draining them, as Marxists would see it, of their ability to see deeper sources of their problems.

A good illustration of the Marxist view is provided by William Sylvis, the leader of the Iron Molders' International Union and later, in the 1860s, head of the National Labor Union. As reported by the monetary historian Irwin Unger in his work, *The Greenback Era* (1964), Sylvis confessed: "For twenty years, I have been trying to discover some remedy for the great wrongs imposed upon labor—to find the reasons why a small portion of the population enjoyed ninety percent of the wealth of the nation, while

the many whose labor produced everything, lived in poverty and want."
He found it in high interest rates and a defective monetary system. "Interest acts like a tax-gatherer; it enters into all things and eats up the price of labor. . . . It produces nothing; all it does is to transfer the products of labor to the pockets of the money lenders, bankers and bondholders." A few years later, Sylvis, still thinking along the same lines, wrote, "when a just monetary system has been established, there will no longer exist a necessity for Trade Unions." Marxists and other socialists would say that there is no better example of how a monetary panacea can distort the thinking of a labor leader—and ultimately the workers themselves.

Socialism Accepted and Rejected

The weakness of socialism and communism in America can also be traced to the preemption of socialist programs by others. Capitalism has responded positively to socialist protests when it has run into difficulties of its own and encountered strong pressures for change. Accordingly, it has reformed itself, as during the years of Wilsonian liberalism, Roosevelt's New Deal, and more recently in wars on poverty, the founding of Medicare, and civil rights legislation. In the 1930s, the New Deal reforms made both socialism and communism much less attractive. When deep trouble has come, capitalism has often been able to adapt itself to the new conditions.

These episodes of social transformation have led a few voices to assert that the question of socialism's weakness is absurd, for the simple reason that America *is* a socialist society. America has adopted, it is said, just about every demand that socialists have ever made over the years. Socialist parties may not have captured the voters directly, but they have been tremendously successful in inducing the major parties to accept their programs. The evidence lies in the country's progressive taxes, the huge welfare system, the strength of labor, and the powerful role of government in almost every area of the economy. Although there is some truth to these allegations with regard to the immediate demands of socialist parties, they cannot be sustained when it comes to the core elements of Marxist-socialism (as discussed in Chapter 2). These elements include working-class control of the state and its agencies, the nationalization of industries, and a strong central planning apparatus.

Finally, in more recent decades, socialism has received a bad name among large numbers of Americans owing to the particular form it has taken in the Soviet Union, Eastern Europe, and Cambodia. Although Marxists would expect capitalist accounts of Soviet society to be distorted, it is nevertheless true that the Soviet experience has proved distasteful not only to the recipients of capitalist versions of Soviet life but also to many who defended the Soviets for a number of years and who are more or less immune to such reports; it has apparently proved distasteful to a sizable number of

Soviet citizens as well. So, for many, the societies in the Soviet bloc have given socialism a black eye.

Capitalism's Antidotes to the Socialist Poison

Although anticapitalist movements in the United States have exhibited many of the characteristics of their British and European counterparts, including class-conscious struggles by the working classes, violence, proliferation of radical dogmas, and much else, nonetheless socialism, and especially its Marxist variant, has had tougher sledding in the United States than across the Atlantic. As we have seen, American socialism enjoyed popularity for only the few decades surrounding the turn of this century and for several years during the Great Depression of the 1930s, but Marxism itself at no time was a potent force in this country.

America's golden age of socialism, during the first two decades of this century, was fashioned not only by the economic conditions of the times but also by a utopian work, Looking Backward *(1887), by the New Englander Edward Bellamy (1850–1898). This book, which sold a million copies in the first few years, relates the story of Julian West, who wakes in the year 2000 from a hypnotically induced sleep begun in 1887 to find that cooperation had replaced competition in all phases of American life and for that reason had brought about miraculous changes. This new society had evolved from the historical tendency of capital to become more and more concentrated in fewer hands, until the state simply took control of the instruments of production and distribution, operating them in the interest of all the citizens. The workers were members of the Industrial Army, working only from the age of twenty-one to that of forty-five and then retiring to intellectual and spiritual enjoyments. All workers received the same pay and so they labored for the social interest, not for personal material gains. The Industrial Army was to maintain the community just as the military army was to protect it.*

In this new society of the year 2000, there was no buying and selling, for such activity "is essentially anti-social in all its tendencies. It is an education in self-seeking at the expense of others." The society used no money or gold (but credit cards were employed!), and there were no merchants or bankers. The Industrial Army produced the goods, which were distributed directly from national storehouses. A national planning system brought order to a previously chaotic scramble by profit-seeking individuals, efficiency replacing waste. Julian West declared that waste came from greed, selfishness, destructive competition, and from the private-profit enterprise system.

The movements based on Bellamy's book introduced large numbers of people to socialist ideas—even though Bellamy himself scorned the term socialism, for he thought that it reminded people of "atheism, revolution, and sexual novelties." These movements nudged the middle class into the struggle for public ownership, and they contributed to the later attacks against the trusts. They also opened people's eyes to the abuses of the present system, including exploitation of child labor, overpricing by private utilities, adulterated foods, and the power of the "plutocracy," and so they induced many to work for their correction.

For Marxists, however, the Bellamy phenomenon was just another instance of how a mishmash of liberalism could lead people astray. Marxists saw the movement as involving primarily America's middle class—the cultured and conservative class, as Bellamy called it—that was frightened in the late 1870s and the 1880s by the fiery class struggles going on all around them. Bellamy's message, which Marxists disdained, was that these struggles would eventually give way to unity, affluence for all, perfection of institutions—to the new society.

The causes of Marxism's debility in the United States are probably traceable, first of all, to the fact that capitalism was, in a sense, transplanted in America, obviating its need to overcome a feudal aristocracy through protracted class struggles (slavery and the Civil War notwithstanding), and that the transplantation occurred in a land of tremendous potential wealth that allowed upward social and economic mobility for great numbers of its citizens. These factors combined to minimize class differences and to enhance the chances for any part of the population to gain without having to take something away from others.

Second, the people who came to America possessed an astonishing diversity of racial, cultural, and religious backgrounds, and many of them were fleeing persecution, repression, or societies that forced them into economic cul-de-sacs. These Old World repulsions generated in America a large percentage of the population with characteristics of extreme individualism, distrust of authority, and deep suspicions of others. Such a population, situated in a land of potential abundance, increasingly inculcated with an ideology that stressed "making it on one's own," was not the raw material out of which a collectivist movement could be fashioned.

Third, though socialism did at times make some headway despite these handicaps, its strength was constantly dissipated among an astounding assortment of anticapitalist and reformist movements, each of which drew some energy from the others, and all of which suffered as a result. This pronounced tendency of socialism to diversify, fracture, and disintegrate was caused not only by the factors already discussed but also by the particular way that U.S. capitalism developed, which created new objective conditions, erased old ones, and produced one opportunity after another (even though illusory for some) for workers to improve their lot. Capitalism's recurrent financial disorders also weakened socialism by attracting large numbers of workers to movements promising happiness and wealth through monetary nostrums.

Finally, the periodic and often severe crises generated by capitalist development compelled the capital-owning classes to appropriate many of the immediate demands of their adversaries. This strategy was at times supplemented by direct action against the more dangerous elements of the population.

In sum, communism made little headway in Western Europe and America during the nineteenth and early twentieth centuries principally because capitalism created a series of antidotes against the Marxist poison. Having created Marxism itself, capitalism then turned on "its monster" with diverting sideshows, divisive flourishes, radical competitors, deadly potions, and modern technology. Most of these weapons were fashioned within the normal growth processes of the capitalist mode of production itself. Thus, Marxism came from the womb of capitalism and it was enfeebled, not by external forces, but by the natural juices of its own mother.

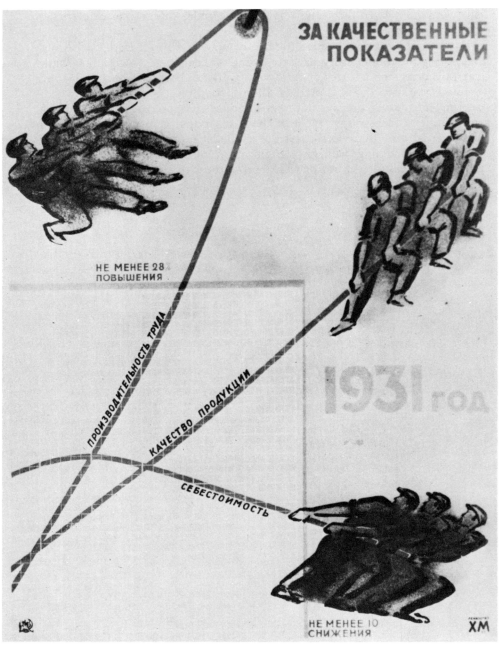

A Soviet industrial productivity poster (1931) exhorting workers to achieve an increase in labor productivity of at least 28 percent, an upswing in the quality of production, and a reduction of costs of at least 10 percent. (Mueller and Graeff Collection, Hoover Institution Archives)

4

Initial Successes of Communism in Russia, China, and Elsewhere

INDUSTRIAL CAPITALISM NOT ONLY SPAWNED revolutionary Marxism, which in theory and practice became capitalism's principal antagonist, but it also brought forth the conditions that led to the early defeat of its enemy in the advanced areas of the world. All this we have seen. In this chapter, we shall see how the evolution of capitalism also created a global environment that served to advance the success of communist revolutions in Russia, China, and other less-developed areas of the world.

The Expectations of Marx and Engels

Marx expected the first proletarian revolutions to take place in the advanced capitalist countries of Western Europe and North America. He based this expectation on his materialist conception of history, from which he concluded, "No social order ever perishes before all the productive forces for which there is room in it have developed." It followed that: "The country that is more developed industrially only shows to the less developed, the image of its own future."

In 1858, in a letter to Engels, Marx indicated that Western Europe would shortly become socialist, which suggested to him that, with the rest of the world expanding the capitalist way, such socialism would be endangered. Explaining this, Marx wrote: "The difficult question for us is: on the Continent the revolution is imminent and will immediately take a socialist character. Is it not bound to be crushed in this little corner, considering that in a far greater territory the movement of bourgeois society is still in the ascendent?" Marx also criticized Michael Bakunin, the Russian anarchist, for relying on "will power and not economic conditions [as] the basis of his social revolution." Engels attacked the Russian revolutionist, Petr

Tkachev, for much the same thing. Revolutions, Engels wrote, are not made to order like a piece of flowered calico. One does not simply start shooting at three or four places simultaneously and expect the people to be liberated and the country transformed into a model socialist society. No. Both Marx and Engels believed that a large, class-conscious proletariat would first have to be formed, with wealth highly concentrated and poverty widespread, before conditions were ripe for a successful revolution. Such seasoning could be achieved only when the country had raised its production to high levels, and when further gains in production were prevented by outmoded institutions and practices.

As Marx visualized the process, socialist economic development in Europe would be rationally planned instead of being ruled by the "blind forces of nature." Beyond that stage lies what Marx called "the true realm of freedom" in which, enough material production having been assured, people no longer work out of necessity but instead fulfill themselves through work as an end in itself.

As for the rest of the world, in Marx's view some countries such as India would proceed through the entire capitalist stage, others perhaps would take shortcuts to socialism—for example, Russia—and still others such as China and some African countries would continue for some time to be mired in precapitalist formations, including especially the "Asiatic mode of production." Marx believed that this mode was characterized by a despotic centralized state power and, beneath it, self-sufficient villages that combined agriculture and manufacturing; the absence of private property in land; and no internal mechanisms of change. Even those countries moving through capitalism would be able to proceed quickly through that stage because they could import the needed technology from the more advanced countries.

In Russia, many scholars believed that their traditional village (the *obshchina*) was unique in its egalitarian and communal institutions and, hence, a foundation on which socialism could be built. In these villages, land was held in common but was periodically redistributed among the peasants for individual family cultivation. Both Marx and Engels thought that the traditional village "might be" the basis for socialism, if proletarian revolutions occurred first in Europe. Countries having such revolutions would be willing and able to provide Russia with the capital goods necessary for transforming the traditional village into a modern socialist agricultural community.

In 1882, in a letter to Karl Kautsky, the leading German Marxist, Engels added some thoughts about the rest of the world. India, he surmised, would carry out a revolution for independence from Great Britain, and the British workers, having come to power, would have to follow their principles and let the revolution run its course. Once Europe and North America become socialist, Engels wrote, they will exert such colossal power and such an example that the less-developed countries will set out on their own paths to socialism. But Engels could not say exactly what those paths would be like. Thus, Engels, unlike Marx, apparently saw no danger of the "little corner" of socialist Europe being crushed by the rising tides of capitalism surrounding it. Indeed, Engels was uncertain about the exact form this rising tide would take.

In short, Marx and Engels expected that Europe would become socialist and pass through the "realm of necessity" into the "realm of freedom." The class domination by the workers, through the state, would last "until the economic foundations of the existence of classes are destroyed." Socialist Europe would withdraw from colonial endeavors. The rest of the world would have a variety of possibilities. Some countries would continue through a capitalism that had been imposed on them by colonial powers. Others might be able to "leap" into socialism without the full capitalist experience. Still others, untouched by colonialism, would remain immobile for some time in precapitalist formations. Eventually, however, in one way or another, all would arrive at socialism.

In fact, however, the actual situation became almost the exact opposite of what Marx and Engels envisaged. Proletarian revolutions did not occur in Western Europe and North America. Instead, the first Marxist revolutions took place in the less-developed areas of the world. Instead of an expanding capitalism in the rest of the world threatening socialism "in this little corner," an expanding Marxism throughout much of the less-developed world became a threat to the stability of European and American capitalism.

The Spread of Communism in the Twentieth Century

Marx and Engels warned in the *Communist Manifesto* (1848) that the specter of communism was haunting Europe, where, as we have seen, they fully expected the first proletarian revolutions to occur. Although they later modified these expectations in a number of ways, their hopes about such uprisings were retained to the end. During the last decade or so of Marx's life, he did speculate about the possibility of a socialist transformation in Russia. He noted in a letter of 1880 that in Russia "*Das Kapital* [his major work] is more read and appreciated than anywhere else."

Marxism, as an organization, arrived in Russia during the 1880s, gradually built itself up during the next decade, and in the beginning years of the twentieth century became a formidable revolutionary movement. The Bolshevik wing of this movement, led by Lenin, finally succeeded in October 1917 in carrying out the first communist revolution in the world.

Lenin (1870–1924) was born in Simbirsk, which lies on the Volga River over 350 miles southeast of Moscow. When he was seventeen, his older brother, a Marxist, was hanged for plotting the assassination of Tsar Alexander III. Shortly after that, Lenin turned to Marxist literature, which eventually led him into revolutionary activities in St. Petersburg. He was jailed in late 1895 for such activities and exiled a year later to Siberia for three years. Afterward, he traveled to European capitals to contact Russian revolutionary exiles and to involve himself in their work. He helped to launch revolutionary periodicals that were smuggled into Russia, and he organized the Bolshevik wing of the Social Democratic party.

He returned to Russia in 1905 to participate in the revolution that erupted that year in St. Petersburg, Moscow, and other Russian cities and villages. After the revolutionaries were defeated, Lenin settled in Switzerland and did not return to Russia until April 1917. He spent these years in Geneva, Paris, Cracow, and Zurich writing revolutionary documents and plotting for the overthrow of the tsarist regime.

Russia's agony in World War I finally led to revolts against the regime in February 1917. The tsar abdicated in the following month, and a provisional government was established. Lenin left Zurich in April for Petrograd (formerly St. Petersburg), and immediately began organizing the Bolsheviks for the overthrow of the new government. The Bolsheviks succeeded in this aim in October 1917. Lenin became the president of the Soviet of People's Commissars and led his people in the civil war with the counterrevolutionary White armies. After the Bolsheviks' victory, Lenin turned his attention to the economic development of the country.

However, during December 1921, he became seriously ill and was unable to work for several weeks. Between May 1922 and March 1923 he suffered three strokes, the second removing him from effective leadership of the government, and the third from public life. He lingered on for ten months after his third stroke, dying on January 21, 1924, at the age of fifty-three.

In November 1924, the People's Republic of Mongolia became the second Marxist state, supported by the young Soviet Union. Then for the next twenty years or so Marxism added no new states to its roster. World War I contributed importantly to the first (and indirectly to the second) Marxist government by creating the appalling conditions in Russia that brought the masses to a state of desperation and that made it impossible for the autocracy to continue to rule. War casualties, destruction, and famine cleared the field for the occupation of communism. Similarly, World War II established the conditions for another red wave. Part of this wave broke forth in Eastern Europe, where a few indigenous Marxist movements (in Albania and Yugoslavia) succeeded in overthrowing old regimes without Soviet assistance, and where Soviet pressure and its military might produced revolutionary transformations elsewhere in this area. Another part of the red wave broke in Asia, where the Chinese Communist party attained its objective in October 1949; a Marxian government was founded in North Korea on May 1, 1948; and fluid and unstable portions of Vietnam were under communist and nationalist control immediately after World War II. (These conditions in Vietnam continued throughout the years of French [1946–54] and later American [1961–73] military involvement. A few years

A Russian poster commemorating Bloody Sunday, which triggered the first Russian Revolution, in 1905. Hundreds were killed when the imperial guards opened fire on peasants who had gathered outside the Winter Palace to petition the czar, to tell him of their hardships and pray for his help. (New York Public Library Picture Collection)

after the American forces pulled out of Vietnam in 1973, a communist government for the entire country took power.) Consequently, by 1950, there were twelve Marxist states in the world, possessing over 30 percent of the world's population and a quarter of the world's land area.

During the 1950s and 1960s only one new Marxist government was added to the communist camp, that of Cuba. Fidel Castro and his followers captured political control there in early 1959 and about two years later declared themselves to be Marxists and in alliance with the Soviet Union.

The 1970s and the early years of the next decade witnessed a third wave of Marxist victories, which spread all the way from Southeast Asia, through one state in South Asia, on through a small piece of the Arabian peninsula and large parts of Africa, and on into a few islands and states of the Caribbean and Central America. Altogether, there are now about two dozen countries with Marxist governments. These countries produce a fifth of the world's gross national product, occupy about a third of its land area, and possess over a third of its population. In addition, strong Marxist political parties exist in several other countries around the world, including France, Italy, and India.

The Soviet Union and China dominate the communist camp—in population, economic and military power, and territory. Moreover, the Soviet revolution established the pattern for communism in Mongolia and Eastern Europe, and to a lesser extent in North Korea, while both the Soviet and the Chinese revolutions were the necessary backdrop for later communist successes in Southeast Asia. These communist giants have also, by pressure and example, strongly influenced communist revolutions elsewhere.

Why Marxism Succeeded First in Russia

Having been thwarted in the advanced world, why was Marxism able to establish itself in the less-developed world, and why, in particular, in Russia first of all?

We have seen that Marx and Engels were wrong in their belief that, in general, countries would attain socialism only after capitalism had been fully developed. In many ways, capitalism as it matures gains strength against socialist forces, so that if Marxist socialism is to triumph against capitalism, it has its best opportunity to do so in the earlier stages of capitalist development. This means that, once capitalism has matured in the leading industrial countries, Marxism has to find its way into the less-developed areas of the world.

Frequently, the colonial powers had imposed their rule in the poorer countries in ways that inhibited self-sustaining economic development by these lesser nations. For example, autocratic ruling classes, firmly opposed to the radical changes that accompany self-generated economic development, were often supported by foreign capitalists and their governments, who together endeavored to maintain stable and favorable investment and political climates. Often local capitalists were hindered in developing their own operations fully when foreign capitalists entered the local markets with superior technology, lower-cost goods, and better marketing arrangements. Colonial powers frequently disrupted the production patterns of local economies in order to transform them into suppliers of certain raw materials for the advanced economies or certain products for export markets. The foreign powers extracted valuable natural resources and other wealth from the colonized areas and had an interest in keeping local labor as cheap and as unorganized as possible.

In general, foreign capitalists and their governments acted in the poorer areas in ways that aided the advanced areas much more than they helped the poorer ones. These policies generated opposition to imperialism and to the local ruling classes that were supported by foreign capital, which prepared the ground for strong nationalist and Marxist revolutionary movements. In addition, many revolutionary opportunities were opened up when the capitalist powers fought each other in the two world wars, as we shall discuss later.

Therefore, once it had been denied the throne in the advanced countries, revolutionary Marxism found conditions much more receptive in the less-developed areas. With great effectiveness, Marxists could point to the enervating influences on local economies of foreign capitalists and local feudalism, and many of their explanations of why so many people were poor and miserable in these areas rang true to a good many ears.

But why was Russia, in particular, the starting point of Marxist revolution? First of all, the odds were extremely low that a successful Marxist revolution at that time could occur in a small country, for most of these were part of the colonial domain of an imperial power. Few underdeveloped nations had an independent status.

Furthermore, it took a long time for revolutionary Marxism to become widely and correctly known and to spread from its birthplace to other areas of the world. At the time of the First World War, Marxism was virtually unheard of in most of what we today call the Third World—Asia, Africa, and Latin America. For example, probably only a few Chinese intellectuals had ever heard of Marxism by 1910, and the same is true for India, Brazil, Mexico, and Southeast Asia; Africa was almost a complete blank in this regard. In those years, Marxism was known outside of its birthplace of Western Europe and England only in those countries that had easy access, by way of travel and emigration, to the sources of such ideas.

Russia's sporadic efforts to learn from the West, involving movements of Russian intellectuals back and forth between the two areas, and European emigration to America, sent Marxism east and west to those lands. It did not travel elsewhere. Consequently, if the initial Marxist revolution was not to occur in any of the advanced capitalist nations, and if it was to occur somewhere else at a relatively early stage of development, then only a few candidates were in the running—Eastern Europe and Russia.

A Marxist revolution has the best chance to succeed, as Marx, Engels, Lenin, and others recognized, where the ruling classes have been weakened to the degree that they are no longer able to govern effectively. The First World War, which Marxists viewed as a global conflict among the capitalist powers for the redivision of the world, proved so devastating to most of the major participants, and of course especially to the major losers, that conditions were laid for an overturn of the societies that had failed their citizens so thoroughly. To Lenin and others, the ruling classes in the defeated countries had lost their ability to govern effectively.

The countries most battered by the war were Russia, Germany, and the Austro-Hungarian monarchy (the Hapsburg empire). In all of these areas, Marxist uprisings occurred, but the Bolshevik revolution in Russia came first and the others followed partly in response to the Russian upheaval. In Hungary, Communists seized power in March 1919, but they were defeated a few months later by internal opposition and by the invasion of Rumanian armed forces, which were hostile to the radical government next door. Germany was exhausted to the point of collapse and faced the harsh peace terms laid down at Versailles. These conditions opened the way for a series of communist uprisings—the Spartacist revolt in early 1919, which was brutally suppressed, and further Marxist bids for power in 1921 and 1923, both of which were rather easily turned back.

The Russian masses were terribly battered by the war, and the tsarist regime was near collapse by the end of it. Hardship and hunger were rampant; strikes and riots spread throughout the land. In early 1917 the tsarist government was overthrown, and the liberal bourgeoisie took power. But the Bolsheviks gathered strength in the following months until, in October, this Marxist party had garnered so much support in the capital, and the liberal bourgeois government had become so isolated, that Lenin and his followers were able to claim power with little opposition. This first Marxist revolution could not be undone, for it occurred in a land that was simply too massive to allow decisive counteraction by the capitalist powers. The revolution occurred in Russia and not in China, India, or elsewhere because it was only the Russian regime that was thoroughly discredited, and it was the Russian masses and not the peoples of those other countries who were crushed in the First World War. That capitalist war, by weakening the top and inflaming the bottom, led to the Bolsheviks' conquest.

Other historical conditions and events in Russia contributed as well to form the basis for the victory of Marxism in that country. In nineteenth-century Russia, a dispute took place between a group known as the Westernists and another called the Slavophiles. The Westernists believed that Russia's future development would depend on the adoption of Western technology and social institutions, including representative and liberal government. The basis for these beliefs was the contention that Russia was a part of Europe and so was destined to follow the path already laid out by the more advanced European countries. Many of the adherents of this view looked back to Peter the Great, who reigned from 1689 to 1725, as their herald of a westernizing movement that would break with the more inward-looking policies of the past.

The Slavophiles, opposed to these views, contended that Russian civilization was unique and superior to those of the West, because it was based on the Orthodox Church, the traditional village, the ancient popular assembly of Kievan Russia (from the tenth to the thirteenth centuries), and the love that binds the people to the tsar. Russia, they held, would not follow the West but would, instead, look to its own traditions and, by so doing, achieve a civilization that would supersede that of Europe. The Slavophiles looked backward to medieval Russia, but at the same time supported individual liberty, equality, brotherhood, and the termination of serfdom. They expressed faith in the collective institutions and cooperative endeavors of the peasants—and, indeed, in the peasants themselves—focusing attention on the distinctive character of the Russian way of life within the traditional village.

The Populist movement of the 1860s in Russia built on the views of the Slavophiles. The Populists argued that Russia could largely leap past industrial capitalism by immediately constructing socialism on the basis of the Russian village with its traditions of equality, collective ownership of land, and communal self-government; these villages, they thought, could be held together by a loose voluntary confederation that would replace the state. The Populists' central goals were social justice and social equality. They claimed that haste was necessary to achieve these aims, for capitalism was already developing rapidly in Russia. These views led to an active revolutionary strategy in Russia, to the formation of parties to which professional conspirators dedicated their lives, all of which the tsarist regime further encouraged by its repressive responses. The Populists evolved into a People's party and the party of the People's Will—the latter intent on direct attacks against the political structure, including regicide. After these movements faded, the Populist creed reappeared later in the views of the Socialist Revolutionary party, which was formed in 1901 as a militant version of resurgent populism.

The rural focus of these Russian radicals was quite foreign to traditional, urban-based Marxism, but it became essential for Marxism to incorporate the Populist point of view into its theory and practice once Marxism was compelled to move from the advanced to the less-developed areas of the world. Thus, Marxism found in Russian populism exactly what it needed to propel it forward in such an alien climate.

Lenin integrated orthodox Marxism and Russian Populist views into a new version of Marxism—later known as Marxism-Leninism—which included a revolutionary role for the peasantry in a two-stage drama of revolt. The Russian radical movements of the nineteenth century also gave Lenin the ingredients for his innovative organization, the vanguard communist party, which the Bolshevik leader insisted should be a tightly knit and secretive party of professional revolutionaries. This party of knowledgeable Marxists would impart the theory of Marxist socialism to the workers, who otherwise would have been concerned only with questions of wages and working conditions. As we have seen, Lenin intended for the party to lead the workers to revolution, and, after that, to lead the country as a whole along the path to socialism and communism.

The activism that Marxism encountered in Russia was in sharp contrast to the passivity that had all but immobilized European Marxist movements up to that time. In Europe, socialists believed more and more that capitalism had to run its full course before a socialist revolution could succeed, and that in the long meantime Marxists should be patient and seek to improve the lives of the working classes, gradually building up their and the workers' strength for that future day of reckoning. Lenin's contribution was to restore will, action, and initiative into a Marxism that was simply standing by—awaiting the inexorable forward march of history.

Lenin succeeded in carrying out a revolution with Populist timing—that is, before the full development of capitalism had taken place—but with Marxist justification. Lenin justified this cataclysmic event in Marxist terminology, and in fact it owed much to Marxist theory and practice, but the revolution was also a culmination of Russia's own history.

Why Marxism Succeeded in China

Having seen why Marxism's first revolutionary victory occurred in Russia, now let us examine why its next major victory was in China.

As noted earlier, European industrial capitalism during the nineteenth century evolved into what Lenin called its monopoly and imperialist stage— a stage in which large financial and industrial enterprises sought profitable overseas outlets for their capital and markets for their goods. National governments of the capitalist powers protected these investments and markets with political and military means. It was a stage of capitalist development, Lenin said, during which the capitalist powers divided up the world economically and politically, with Great Britain and France gaining most of "the pie," but some of it also going to Italy, Germany, Belgium, the United States, Japan, and others.

China felt the imperialist blows during the last several decades of the nineteenth century and the early decades of the twentieth. Great Britain, France, and other capitalist powers repeatedly used force against the Chinese in attempts to open China to profit making. The British endeavored to extend their lucrative opium exports to China in exchange for tea and silks, but the Ch'ing (Qing, Manchu) dynasty (1644–1911) had long resisted free and open trade with the West and especially the dangerously expanding opium imports, which were having a debilitating effect on growing numbers of Chinese. This clash of interests culminated in the first Opium War (1839–42), which the British won. The Chinese were compelled to open more ports to foreign trade and residency, and they ceded Hong Kong to the British. Other Western powers received similar privileges within a few years.

In the second Opium War, about fifteen years after the first, the British and French occupied Canton in the south and Tientsin in the north and forced the Chinese into opening more ports, sanctioning Christian missionary activities, and legalizing opium imports. A year later, the two capitalist powers renewed the war, occupied Peking, burned the imperial summer palace, and forced further concessions from the Chinese government. Once again, other Western powers were accorded equal privileges. For the next half century, up to the fall of the dynasty in 1911, China was under siege, yielding territory, granting concessions, incurring large foreign debts, and suffering major military defeats.

The Ch'ing dynasty, Chinese entrepreneurs, and many disturbed citizens responded to these assaults in a sequence of actions that began conservatively but became increasingly radical—that is, increasingly threatening to the stability of China's traditional social structure. China's attempts to fend off the foreigners began with efforts to strengthen its military defenses and its Confucian values—armaments and ideology. The military buildup led to the establishment of supporting mining, transportation, and industrial enterprises. At the close of the nineteenth century, the young emperor and some officials and leading scholars issued a series of reforms, involving the economy, the government, and education. However, these edicts remained largely on paper, and in the end they came to nothing. The ineffectiveness of China's responses to the foreign challenges led others, including Sun Yat-sen (1866–1925), to the belief that China's problems could not be solved unless the Ch'ing dynasty itself was overthrown. These radical elements realized their goal in 1911, when a series of local rebellions against the Manchus occurred that quickly accumulated into a national consensus for the dynasty's removal.

Sun's ideas about the new society to be erected from the rubble of the old were heavily influenced by the West, but they were not always well thought out or consistent. His most popular prescription for the new China was "the three principles of the people," which he said came from Abraham Lincoln's "of the people, by the people, and for the people." Sun translated these as nationalism (later interpreted as anti-imperialism), democracy, and the people's livelihood, which originally meant a reduction of poverty and a curb on the tyrannical and irresponsible use of great wealth (but later came to signify socialism). These prescriptions, however, proved to be largely utopian, divorced from real movements inside and outside of China. They, too, remained merely sketches on paper of how to achieve the new China. The new China was ultimately fashioned not from these musings, but from underlying domestic and world forces that lay outside of Sun's ken.

In the meantime, the United States, which was becoming a power in the Caribbean and the Pacific, "opened" Japan to trade in 1853–54, when Commodore Matthew C. Perry with a show of naval force entered Tokyo Bay. This action started the series of events that led to the fall of the Tokugawa regime (1603–1867), the disintegration of Japan's centralized feudal economy, and the development of the economy along Western lines—that is, industrial and capitalist lines, though with heavy state participation. Before the turn of the century, Japan was fast becoming an industrial and capitalist power complemented by growing military forces. The Japanese, in their first major move as an imperialist nation, fought and beat the Chinese in the war of 1894–95, gaining Formosa and the Pescadores. They defeated the Russians in 1904–5, which led to their presence in Manchuria. Japan then annexed Korea five years later.

Japan's defeat of China contributed heavily to the aborted reforms of 1898 and to the overthrow of the Ch'ing dynasty thirteen years later. Japan's victory over the Russians led immediately to the 1905 revolution in that country, in which Trotsky and Lenin played leading roles. Thus, the expanding military and economic strength of Japan threw both of its neighboring giants into social and political turmoil.

The uneven economic development of the advanced capitalist nations, in which some of them developed into industrial and military powers decades before others, eventually created challengers, such as Germany, to the leading colonial powers, Great Britain and France. This factor, together with the imperial ambitions of all the capitalist powers for new territory, markets, and resources, finally embroiled them in the First World War. The Russian revolution of 1905 and World War I a decade later combined to create chaotic and revolutionary conditions that culminated in the 1917 Bolshevik upheaval.

The 1911 revolution in China and the Bolsheviks' victory prepared the ground for the formation of the Chinese Communist party in 1921. Members of this party a few years later joined forces with Chiang Kai-shek's Nationalist party (the Kuomintang) in an attempt to reunify the country—

The storming of Peking by combined British and French forces in 1860. (The Bettmann Archive, Inc.)

which had broken up after 1911 into a number of regions headed by "war-lords," autonomous regional military commanders. After this collaboration collapsed in 1927 and the Communists were driven out of China's main urban areas, many of them regrouped in the countryside and for the next twenty-two years strengthened their forces by responding to the grievances of peasants with land reforms, rent controls, cooperatives, and other social and economic programs. The ultimate result of these efforts was the victory of the Communists over the Nationalists in the Chinese civil war of 1946–49.

During the beginning decades of the twentieth century, Japan's imperial designs grew bolder as the presence in Asia of the European powers declined, which itself stemmed from the impact of the First World War and the later depressed economic conditions within world capitalism after the Great Crash of 1929 in the United States. In 1931 Japan invaded all of northeast China, penetrated other parts of north China in the next several years, and in 1937 invaded the northern provinces, the coastal areas, and occupied much of the rich Yangtze River valley. By facing the Japanese invaders head-on and appealing to the nationalism of all Chinese, the Communist party was able to build itself into a strong political-military organization. The Second World War, which grew out of the conditions created by the previous conflagration, resulted in Japan's military defeat, and thus opened the way for the triumph of the Communists in China.

Thus, world capitalism itself produced the conditions for a communist victory in China. But Marxism's triumph in China also owed much to the conditions that developed from China's own history. From the late eighteenth century on, the Chinese economy was in deep trouble, for it was not producing enough food for its rapidly expanding population. Harvard economist Dwight Perkins estimated, in *Agricultural Development in China 1368–1968*, that between 1770 and 1913 China's population rose by 60 percent while cultivated acreage increased by only a bit more than 40 percent. During the nineteenth century, the Ch'ing dynasty was repeatedly weakened by famines and rebellions. The Taiping rebellion, which lasted from 1850 to 1864, and which was directly and indirectly responsible for 40 million to 60 million human casualties and much physical destruction of the countryside, came close to toppling the dynasty at that time. Real income for the great majority of Chinese did not rise at all over the entire century, and millions starved to death during periodic famines.

Despite these basic hardships, landlords, officials, moneylenders, and others extracted from peasants and workers much of whatever economic surpluses they managed to produce. These surpluses were largely funneled into luxury consumption, extravagant construction, hoards of inventories, and foreign assets, none of which was useful for the growth of the economy. The government participated in the exploitation and the wasteful spending and protected the social classes involved with it. The peasants above all were ground down to near impotence by the continuing exploitation. Given these conditions, much of Marxism's analysis did not have to come to Chinese workers and peasants from the outside, for they learned about exploitation and class structures from their own experiences.

After the fall of the Ch'ing dynasty, no central authority existed to replace it. As a result, social turmoil was commonplace and persistent. Even after 1927 when Chiang Kai-shek (1887–1975) unified the Republic to some extent, the Chinese were subjected to the pains of the worldwide depression and to the lack of any coherent economic program that could raise the masses from their pitiful levels of subsistence. In short, at the time Marxism appeared on the Chinese scene, in the 1920s, the economy was highly vulnerable and social unrest was widespread.

China was also receptive to Marxism because Chinese philosophical thought and values were, or could be made, compatible with the philosophical outlook of Marxism. Although Mao Zedong and the party rejected much of Confucianism, Buddhism, and Taoism, they could also accept many of China's traditional beliefs. For example, the Taoist formulation of the yin and yang principles, in which opposites, such as female-male and dark-light, confront one another, became an almost perfect backdrop for the Marxists' explanation of the Hegelian and Marxian dialectic. Mao also used the Buddhist and Confucianist strictures on selfishness and greed, the Confucian disparagement of the profit motive, its warning about the seeking of gain and fame, and the traditional Chinese approval of frugal living, modest and sincere behavior, and dedicated toil. These became the virtues of outstanding Communist comrades. China's traditions also exalted agricultural labor and lauded the peasants' innate wisdom and rationality, both of which the Chinese Communist party drew upon heavily.

Mao Zedong (1893–1976) was born in Shaoshan, a village in the province of Hunan in south China. There he went to school and worked on his parents' land until he was seventeen, at which time he entered a middle school in Ch'angsha, the capital of his province. Later in that year, he joined the revolutionary army that shortly overthrew the Ch'ing dynasty, and was discharged in early 1912. He continued his education at a teacher's training school, graduating in 1918 at the age of twenty-four.

In that year he went to Peking for the first time, and there he became a librarian's assistant at Peking University, under Li Ta-chao, who later was a founder of the Chinese Communist party. While at the university, Mao joined a Marxist study group. Returning to Ch'angsha, Mao became director of a primary school and, in his spare time, the organizer of a Communist party in that city. This and similar groups elsewhere were the nuclei of the Chinese Communist party, which was organized in Shanghai, in July 1921, with Mao in attendance. In late 1922, Mao resigned as director of the primary school in order to devote all of his energies to revolutionary activities. He was elected to the Central Committee of his party in 1923, and in the following few years he worked on the problems of peasants, which culminated in 1927 in a brilliant and unforgettable report on the peasant movement in Hunan.

Later in 1927, Mao established a revolutionary base area in the mountains not far from his birthplace. Such bases were established elsewhere by others in the party. These soviet areas, as they were called, were under almost constant military attack from the Kuomintang forces. Finally in 1934, after four years of encirclement campaigns, the armies of Chiang Kai-shek drove the Communists from their base areas and forced them into the Long March to the northwest of the country. This famous event began in October 1934 and ended a year later when Mao's group arrived in Shensi province, several hundred miles southwest of Peking. In this area, centered around Yenan, Mao and others reestablished their base areas. By this time, Mao was the leader of the Chinese Communist party.

The Japanese began their all-out attack on China in 1937, and for much of the time during the next eight years the Communists were engaged in fighting the invaders. Shortly after the Japanese surrender to the Allies in 1945, civil war between the Communists and Chiang Kai-shek's forces began in earnest, the Communists gaining victory in 1949. On October 1 of that year, Mao, in Peking, proclaimed the founding of the People's Republic of China and was elected chairman of the Republic.

Mao led his nation through the Korean War, the Great Leap Forward, the Cultural Revolution, and a series of economic development programs until his death.

Marxism, therefore, found both the economic conditions and the value system to be friendly hosts when it landed on China's doorstep after the First World War. Many Chinese, out of misery, sought radical change, and they were offered a doctrine that often rang true to their deepest beliefs.

Marxism's Initial Successes Elsewhere

As the advanced capitalist countries expanded to create empires on a global basis, revolutionary movements in the poorer countries of the world were formed against them. As we saw in Chapter 1, these revolutionary efforts were more complex than those envisaged in classical Marxism. Whereas the theory of revolution in the advanced capitalist areas had required only the uprising of a massive urban proletariat, the attainment of socialism in the underdeveloped areas required alliances among several classes and leadership by a vanguard communist party.

Many of the communist revolutions in the less-developed areas owe their success to capitalism's two world wars. The Russian and Chinese revolutions would have been long delayed, at best, without those wars. Communism in Eastern Europe owes its existence in large part to the turbulent conditions created in that region by the Second World War, and the same is true for North Korea and Southeast Asia. World War II dissolved old colonial empires, weakened existing ruling classes, raised nationalism to a high pitch, and thus opened the way for new alignments of political forces, including communists. With the Russian Revolution coming out of the First World War and the Chinese Revolution out of the Second, it is not surprising that the Second World War also produced a clustering of smaller communist nations around the two giants. These border clusterings appeared because the giant communist countries found it in their interest and competence to give moral, tactical, military, and economic assistance to Marxists and to other radical groups in those lands, and because many of the local conditions there were similar to those that contributed to the revolutions in the nearby giant countries.

Beyond that, communist revolutions have succeeded in areas where old colonial powers have persisted in wielding political and economic power over subject populations long after many peoples of the world had liberated themselves or been given their freedom—and for too long to retain the good will of native populations. This set of forces largely accounts for successful communist revolutions in Guinea-Bissau, Angola, and Mozambique, which the Portuguese held onto long enough to foment revolt against them. It also helps to explain the success of Marxism and radicalism in Zimbabwe, where white settlers attempted to retain their political power indefinitely and, by so doing, forced their black opponents into increasingly radical positions. Cuba, too, falls into this pattern, where the United States had long been the dominant foreign influence, supporting an increasingly unpopular regime during the 1950s. This set of forces has also contributed to the successful Marxist revolutions in Southeast Asia, where the French fought for years to continue their colonial rule, and where the Americans, after the defeat of the French, fought for more than a decade to prevent a communist victory. Marxism also gained a foothold in Southern Yemen, after the British ended their long domination of the region in the late 1960s. Nicaragua provides another example: The United States for years supported the corrupt Somoza family, which fell in 1979 to a coalition government with strong Marxist elements. All of these examples are in sharp contrast to the experience in India, to which the British granted independence early enough to avoid the radicalization of ever-larger numbers of nationalists.

The Giants Weakened

The way capitalism developed as a world system aided in establishing the conditions for successful Marxist-Leninist revolutions in the less-developed areas. The resultant rapid spread of communism across the continents has, as we shall see, challenged and weakened world capitalism. At the same time, however, world communism, after its successful revolutions, has not found a route to attractive and vigorous socialist societies. Revolutions are one thing; the attainment of socialism is something else. Thus, two giants face each other, each partly responsible for what it sees, and each weakened from their combined efforts.

The final bells toll at the New York Stock Exchange, November 4, 1982, the heaviest day of trading in the 190-yea history of the exchange. More than 149 million shares changed hands. (Ralph Morse—TIME Magazine)

5

The Elusive Strength of Capitalism

ON MANY OCCASIONS DURING THE PAST CENTURY, Marxists have thought that capitalism was down for the count. This mode of production has survived some hard knocks and bloody internecine battles, and there have been times when it did appear to be on its last legs. Yet it has always come back with renewed strength.

Marx and Engels themselves remarked as long ago as 1848 how amazing were the accomplishments of the bourgeoisie "during its rule of scarce one hundred years." What earlier centuries, they asked, "had even a presentiment that such productive forces slumbered in the lap of social labor?" Much the same could have been said on numerous occasions later on. Still, these two revolutionists went on to predict the ultimate end of capitalist society, and Marxists after them have kept to that faith. The faith was briefly joined with hope during the Paris Commune in 1871, the depressed years of the 1890s, again during the First World War and the immediate aftermath of the Russian Revolution, once again during the Great Depression of the 1930s, and still later in the Second World War. Marxists have predicted the demise of capitalism during each of its sharp declines into recession or depression. At each of these junctures, the question reappears: Has capitalism reached the end of the line? Or will it pull itself together for still another surge forward?

How strong is world capitalism? It is extremely difficult to assess the health of an entire economic system. The problem is compounded several times over when the system under scrutiny is a global one. It seems brazen even to raise the question. Yet, the question is so important that even a crude answer should be worthwhile. In any case, it is a question we must answer if we are to assess the principal challenges to communism in the world.

First, let us examine the recent evolution of capitalism and some of the impressive accomplishments of this economic system. This examination can stand as a reminder to us that capitalism has had a brilliant past, it continues to enjoy many successes, and its future might be just as radiant, despite signs suggesting otherwise.

The Evolution of Capitalism and Its Accomplishments

Industrial capitalist societies are found today in Western Europe, North America, Australasia, Japan, and a few other places such as Hong Kong, Singapore, South Africa, and Israel. Altogether, they number about twenty-five countries and produce two-thirds of the world's gross national product, while occupying only a quarter of the world's land area and claiming only a fifth of its population. In terms of population, wealth, and world influence, the dominant capitalist countries are the United States, Japan, West Germany, France, and the United Kingdom. These five countries alone produce half of the world's output of goods and services, and they probably possess at least two-thirds of the world's industrial capacity. These five, by their economic performances, can set the world's industrial course.

Four Lines of Advance

Capitalist societies have evolved over the centuries along four main lines of advance. First, they have grown from agricultural and commercial economies to industrial ones, and in recent years the services sector of most of them has become more important than their industrial sector, a development that economists call a postindustrial stage. In days gone by, most people were farmers, small shopkeepers, and traders. Today, the majority of advanced capitalism's labor force work for industry, government, and the private services sector. Self-employment has largely disappeared; almost all workers are now wage earners.

Second, the ownership and control of capital goods (nonresidential structures, producers' durable equipment, and land) have become concentrated in fewer hands. In former days, capitalism was characterized by many small competitive enterprises and only a few giants. Agriculture, commerce, and industry generally consisted of a myriad of tiny capital accumulations, interspersed by a few larger units. At the present time, the advanced capitalist countries are noted for their extraordinarily large industrial and financial corporations, many of which operate on a global scale. By contrast, many of the smaller firms are crowded together in the highly competitive and technologically less-advanced sectors of the economy, such as construction, retail trade, and the services provided by restaurants, hotels, grocery stores, and an assortment of small shops. However, a few of the most progressive areas, such as electronics and biotechnology, are populated with small firms, most of which operate at the frontiers of present-day knowledge. Although most of the largest enterprises are privately owned in the advanced capitalist countries, some are owned and managed by government (Renault, British Steel, Air France), and many are regulated by government (telephone, telegraph, water, radio, television).

Third, as noted above, the numbers of wage earners have risen manyfold at the expense of the self-employed, and they have become assembled in ever-larger working units, in keeping with the growing concentration of capital ownership. These trends have contributed importantly to the growth of trade unions and other less formal workers' organizations. Once weak and outlawed, labor unions can now bargain with managers and owners of capital on terms that are much more equal than they were only several decades ago, not to mention the more servile status of labor a century ago. Even in sectors where labor lacks formal organization, employers often are compelled to grant to their workers most or all of the rights obtained by organized labor. Much bargaining power over recent decades has passed from management to labor.

Fourth, central governments have become increasingly implicated in what used to be the strictly private affairs of capitalist enterprises, consumers, and other sectors of the economy. Governments have never been totally removed from economic activity even in the old days when capitalist societies approached or at least aspired to laissez faire status (noninterference of government in the freedom of individuals to choose in all walks of economic life). No advanced capitalist nation today even approaches being a laissez faire economy; all of them, instead, are mixed (state and private) economies, in which welfare functions are often a sizable part of state involvement. Marxists call such economies "state monopoly capitalism."

Thus, the government's economic role today throughout industrial capitalist societies is a potent one. The government is a heavy demander of goods and services, a producer of some of these products, a transferor of incomes from those most heavily taxed to those receiving government aid in various forms, and a regulator of many private markets. From a Marxist perspective, the state's principal concern in these functions is to assure the sustainable and profitable performance of the group of giant industrial and financial corporations that serve as the engines of modern-day capitalist societies. The state, however, is also greatly influenced by the rising authority of labor, consumer-interest groups, environmentalists, and others, and thus it must try to achieve its goal of supporting the largest concentrations of capital while also satisfying some of the countervailing urgings of these other groups.

These four lines of advance of capitalist nations have interacted with one another. For example, the evolution of capitalism from an agricultural to an industrial base called for larger conglomerations of money and real

Table 5-1: Some Key Changes in the U.S. Economy, 1840s through 1970s

	1840s	1870s	1920s	1970s
As a percentage of work force, workers employed in:				
Agriculture, forestry, fishing	66	50	24	4
Manufacturing, mining, construction, transportation, public utilities	19	30	43	34
Services and government	15	13	14	36
Trade, finance, real estate		7	19	26
Percentage of labor force self-employed	>40	35–40	22	6–7
Labor union membership as a percentage of nonfarm workers	0	1	8	25
Percentage of manufacturing assets held by the largest 100 manufacturing corporations			35	48
Government outlays as a percentage of gross national product	2	4	10	32
Government health and income-security expenditures as a percentage of all government outlays	0	1	4	30

Sources: *The Capitalist System*, second edition, Richard C. Edwards, Michael Reich, and Thomas E. Weiskopf, eds. (Englewood Cliffs, New Jersey: Prentice-Hall, 1978), pp. 113, 180; *Economic Report of the President*, 1980; *Historical Statistics of the United States*, Department of Commerce.

capital, which in turn brought individuals and small labor groups into large urban assemblies of workers, thereby facilitating their organization in unions. As growing labor strength confronted managers and owners of ever-larger units of capital, governments were compelled to intervene at various points in the interest of sustaining the capitalist system.

The U.S. Economy: 1840s–1970s

The United States, as the leading capitalist economy today, provides a good illustration of many of the points just made. Table 5-1 records that, over the past century and more, the U.S. economy has moved decisively from an agricultural to an industrial, or postindustrial (services-sector), focus; and within industry in recent decades capital ownership has become more concentrated. With regard to the former trend, over a century ago, two-thirds of the U.S. labor force were employed in agriculture, forestry, and fishing; today those activities employ only 4 percent. Over the same period, industrial (manufacturing, mining, construction, transportation, and public utilities) employment rose to take up much of the slack; even more was taken up by workers moving into private services and government jobs, and into trade, finance, and real estate. With regard to the concentration of capital ownership, this trend is shown in Table 5-1 by the rise in the percentage of total manufacturing assets held by the largest one hundred manufacturing corporations—from 35 percent in the 1920s to 48 percent in the 1970s.

Not only has the labor force moved out of agriculture into industry and services but an accompanying development has been the sharp decline in self-employed workers, who constituted more than 40 percent of the labor force in the mid-1800s, but who are a mere 6 to 7 percent today. This gap has been filled by wage and salaried employees, including managers and administrators. Well over 90 percent of the labor force are now working for others, not for themselves. This is a major aspect of what Marx referred to as the "proletarianization" of the working class, which has occurred in all the advanced capitalist economies.

In the United States, the labor force has become more extensively organized since the latter part of the nineteenth century. Certainly no more than 1 percent of the nonfarm labor force belonged to unions in the 1870s, but today this proportion is around 25 percent, having reached, however, about a third in the early postwar period. We also see in Table 5-1 that, since the 1840s, government outlays have risen sharply as a percentage of U.S. gross national product, from a mere 2 percent to almost a third today. At the same time, more and more of these expenditures have been devoted to providing health care and income security for the working class and others.

The Postwar Strength of Capitalism

All of the advanced capitalist nations display essentially the same trends as those revealed in Table 5-1 for the United States, although, even in these broad areas, many differences do exist among these countries. For example, the percentage of the labor force employed in agriculture varies from 3 to 5 percent in Great Britain, Belgium, and the United States to as high as 13 to 20 percent in Italy, Austria, and Japan. Labor is more extensively organized in Britain and Denmark than it is in the United States and France. Also government expenditures as a proportion of gross national product are much higher in Sweden and the Netherlands than they are in Japan, the United States, and Switzerland. Nevertheless, the similarities are the more striking aspect of the comparisons, and they derive from the fact that the group shares certain major properties that are characteristic of capitalism's mode of development—from agriculture to industry, rural to urban, small to large government, self-employed to wage workers, and increasing concentration in the assembly of labor and capital.

During the fourteen decades from the 1840s through the 1970s, capitalist countries have enjoyed several periods of booming prosperity, such as during most of the 1880s and the 1950s, but they have also suffered through as many episodes of depression, such as several years of the 1870s and the 1890s, and the entire 1930s. The post-World War II period has been world capitalism's best years, for never before have living standards in these countries risen so rapidly and so persistently. The four postwar decades of sustained, though varying and slowing, economic progress have produced astonishing changes in all of these economies. Moreover, during these decades, no serious depressions have occurred, and the financial panics that marked capitalism before the Second World War have been absent.

Nonetheless, as one would expect, some of the industrial capitalist countries have enjoyed better times than others. Japan, Hong Kong, and Singapore experienced especially high growth rates for most of the postwar years, while Britain, New Zealand, and Switzerland lagged far behind. As a group, however, the capitalist countries recorded average annual growth rates of their gross national products during the postwar period of 4.5 to 5.0 percent, which is unprecedented for them.

Technological advances during these years have also been rapid and extensive. These have appeared in computers, communications equipment, health-care aids and equipment, biotechnology, space exploration, military weapons, energy production, land and air transportation, and much else. Scientific progress in basic research has been swift in biology, chemistry, and physics; and some of this progress has found applications in industry. The capitalist world has created an abundance of new industries, new products, and new and improved methods of producing and distributing merchandise.

World capitalism has shown, in many ways and in numerous areas during the postwar period, a remarkable capacity to adjust to changing conditions. It has perhaps been more adaptable and more responsive to fresh conditions over the most recent four decades than at any previous time. This flexibility has been displayed within the enterprise sector, as it has adjusted to new labor conditions, challenging foreign competition, initial blows from the oil-exporting countries, and unexpected sharp turns in government policies. Capitalism's adaptability has also been revealed in the mobility of its working classes—in their readiness to move to new jobs, to take up different lives, and to reschool and retrain themselves. The diversity of government economic policies throughout the capitalist world to meet changing and different circumstances also reflects this flexibility. Cases in point are the Kennedy fiscal policies of the early 1960s to stimulate

Top: Situated south of San Francisco, Silicon Valley is about 60 miles long and between 5 and 15 miles wide. It is home of the world-famous silicon chip, the tiny heart and mind of the electronics industry. Silicon Valley also houses the greatest concentration of small-to-moderately-sized electronics laboratories and related research-and-development firms in the world. (Robert Isaacs) Bottom: Worker assembles a circuit board at Hewlett-Packard, Palo Alto, California. (Lochon—Gamma)

U.S. economic growth, the many policy changes in the Scandinavian countries in recent years to revamp their tax and welfare systems so as to diminish the heavy role of government in these economies, the Thatcher program of the early 1980s to reinvigorate the British economy and rid it of excessive wage demands and high inflation, Japan's rapid adjustments to the oil crises, and the Reagan tax and monetary measures in the United States to defeat inflation and stimulate capital formation.

For four decades, world capitalism has been unscarred by large-scale wars among the leading capitalist countries, and there are few if any indications now that any such wars are in the offing. Japan, the United States, and the Western European countries appear to have found peaceful methods for settling their differences; more cooperation exists among them than at any previous time. More goods, services, and capital flow among these nations than ever before.

Finally, in assessing the strength of capitalism today, it is pertinent to observe that many people in all walks of life throughout the world wish to immigrate into the United States, Canada, France, Britain, and other advanced capitalist nations. Walls, oceans, rivers, and land masses do not appear to discourage the flows of people into these lands. This fact speaks loudly for the claim that capitalism is still vigorous and able to inspire millions of people. Capitalism also has retained the loyalty of most of its own working classes, if this can be judged by the virtual absence of any revolts against the system as such, and by the low rates of emigration from capitalist to noncapitalist countries.

The evidence regarding capitalism's state of health does not lie only on one side of the ledger. Testimony about the robustness of capitalism can be matched by attestations to weaknesses in its basic structure, to the diminution in the vitality of its leading class of capital owners and managers, and to its declining overall performance in recent years. We must now look at this side of the picture.

Marxist Inroads on the Capitalist Domain

In the early years of this century, a handful of the leading capitalist countries either controlled or dominated most of the world. The British and French spread themselves across northern Africa into the eastern Mediterranean and beyond to numerous lands lying between Jordan and India and between India and China. Both the British and French were careful to step around the Dutch and the Portuguese in what is now Indonesia and to fend off competing claims to Chinese territory from Germany, Russia, Japan, and the United States. European powers, led by Britain, France, Portugal, Belgium, and Germany, established their authority over all of accessible Africa (except Liberia and Ethiopia) between 1880 and 1912. The Caribbean and Central America came under the economic authority (occasionally reinforced militarily) of the United States, which also exerted its power in Hawaii, Guam, and the Philippines.

Although South America liberated itself in the first quarter of the nineteenth century from the political domination of Spain and Portugal, most of this area remained economically dependent on the larger powers throughout the rest of that century and into the next. By the early twentieth century, imperial Japan was on the move in Korea, Formosa, the Pescadores, and the southern areas of Manchuria. The British empire reached its height in the late nineteenth and early twentieth centuries when it comprised one-quarter of the world's land area and population.

The First World War, the Bolshevik Revolution, and the Great Depression of the 1930s gravely weakened the colonial empires. The Second World War and the Chinese Revolution accelerated this process of imperial dissolution. Today capitalism's domain is much reduced from its extent several decades ago. Marxist and nonaligned nations have largely replaced the former colonial and semicolonial lands. Capitalism now exercises its authority over a much smaller proportion of the world's people than it did during the heyday of colonial empires.

The global spread of communism in the twentieth century has diminished the force of advanced capitalist countries by reducing their control over the supplies and prices of world resources, removing their unconstrained entry into new markets for their manufactured goods, and diminishing their access to cheap labor. Industrial capitalist countries can, of course, trade with the Second and Third worlds for the raw materials and natural resources they lack, but they now must trade on terms that are established, not by fiat or by capitalist "gunboats," but on terms mostly under the control of the Second and Third world countries themselves. Moreover, First World capitalist countries may be cut off from these supplies during international crises when the goods are desperately needed. Although these capitalist countries can purchase Second and Third world goods at prices that reflect inexpensive labor costs, that is not as profitable as being able directly to employ these workers in ways and on terms that correspond to the best interests, not of the less-developed country itself, but of the foreign capitalist corporations involved.

The dissolution of the colonial empires and the global spread of communism have strengthened both the Second and the Third world nations relative to the developed countries, including especially the advanced capitalist nations. In the last century and the early years of this one, the underdeveloped areas were vulnerable before the economic and cultural incursions, often backed by superior weapons, of the imperial powers. The people of these areas were frequently reassigned to different work that was profitable to the colonial power; they were dispersed and regrouped—all of which isolated them one from another and so reduced their ability to identify themselves with larger cultural traditions, national boundaries, or supporting social classes and tribes.

Now, much has changed in their favor. The leading communist countries have encouraged, aided, or forced many of the Third World countries to break away from their former masters. Third World people now consider themselves to be nationals, to have valuable cultural traditions, and to be capable of controlling their own resources for goals that also are their own. Some countries of the Third World are able to play off the communist side against the capitalist side to their own advantage. Five oil-rich nations joined originally to establish the OPEC cartel (the member nations of which now number thirteen), while others have entered into marketing arrangements to control the supplies and prices of other natural resources of differing importance. Third World countries have gained much independence, self-esteem, and political muscle.

The sweep of Marxism is not solely responsible for this dramatic transformation, but it is difficult to imagine such turnabouts occurring if world capitalism had not been pushed back and restrained by the communist tide.

Marxism's growing presence in the world has raised the costs to capitalism of defending the areas left to it, increased the risks of operating in this reduced space, and induced some of the local partisans to attack capitalism's bases of operations, to kidnap or kill its government and business representatives, and to subject capitalism to many other abuses. Some of the leading capitalist powers have had repeatedly to use their armed forces during the postwar period to defend their interests: in the Taiwan straits, Korea, Southeast Asia, Lebanon, the Dominican Republic, Zaire, Algeria, and elsewhere. Even more important, the growing nuclear arsenal of the Soviet Union has involved some of the capitalist powers, especially the United States, in an expensive and ever-spiraling arms race. These necessities have raised taxes on America's corporations and people so that valuable resources could be transferred from civilian uses to the military. The armed struggles and military preparations against communism have reduced the ability of capital owners to extract and retain profits from their domestic and foreign operations and so have retarded capital formation in America's enterprises and supporting public facilities (transportation and communication systems, research and development, and health and education).

The Working Classes' Reforms of Capitalism

During the past half-century, workers throughout the capitalist nations have become more strongly organized. Even the workers who are not members of labor unions have become increasingly aware of their own bargaining strength and their legal and conventional rights. The gains made by the organized workers have to a considerable extent enabled the others to elevate their own positions.

One consequence of this is that much of labor is no longer inexpensive. Labor is costly to capital owners not only in terms of basic wages but also with regard to pensions, medical care, layoff and promotion agreements, social security payments, holidays, overtime, work rules, and in many other ways. Moreover, new supplies of labor are not as abundant as they once were, when immigrants more copiously entered the United States and Canada, and cheap Mediterranean labor and skilled Eastern European workers flooded the principal Western European countries; when U.S. blacks moved in large waves from southern rural areas to the industrial north; and when Puerto Ricans and others added significantly to labor supplies. Of course, capitalist enterprises continue to tap what they can—Mexicans, northern Africans, southern Europeans, Asians, former colonial natives, and so on. Moreover, if cheap sources of labor are not available at home, capitalist firms have moved willingly into the less-developed areas of the world to find them. These new labor sources are not inconsequential, but they are not flowing anew each year in the volumes that the past has seen.

Another result of labor's intensified force is that the capitalist system can no longer tolerate mass unemployment, as in the 1930s, nor can it allow itself to sustain full employment over long periods of time. Although high unemployment weakens labor's bargaining position, this condition would probably be successfully opposed by the working classes via the political process. Full employment, by contrast, would intensify labor's economic power to such an extent that much higher wages and lower profits would be the results—not pleasing to capital owners and their managers. Therefore, capitalist governments today generally have to operate in the range between these extremes, although the parameters of the range differ from one country to the next.

In any case, each government seeks to maintain sufficient unemployment to keep labor somewhat malleable (the expressed aim, however, being to prevent further inflation), but not so much unemployment as to rub workers' political fur the wrong way. On balance, labor's gathering strength has, by itself, tended to reduce the ability of capitalist enterprises to draw profits from their operations, and so it has hampered capital formation and economic growth. For a time during the postwar period, as we shall see, other factors favorable to profits more than balanced the adverse impact of labor's greater force. Only with the diminution of the favorable trends did the growing power of workers become of crucial importance to capitalism's vitality.

The Refashioning of Capitalism by Consumers and Others

Other opponents, too, have attacked the business community. Increasing numbers of people have become concerned about threats to the quality of their lives. Environmentalists have demanded more open spaces, cleaner air and water, less local development, the prevention or delay of dangerous or undesirable constructions and projects, and better protection of the country's natural endowments. Similar concerns have been translated into growing demands from various consumer-interest groups, which have placed pressures on business enterprises—and on government, too—to improve the products offered to the public. Increasingly, consumers have been able to return defective products to the manufacturers, to collect monetary settlements through courts for damages and injuries incurred from dangerous products, to demand truthfulness in advertising and in interest charges and other terms of loans, and to reduce the extent of price fixing and other obstacles to competition in retailing. Capital owners and managers, and governmental units that side with them, now confront an increasingly aware and impatient public. One important result of this clash of interests has been to render profit making more difficult owing to the rise of production and litigation costs, the delay of capital investments, and the increase in risks associated with many business and government decisions. The capital-owning classes, therefore, have been weakened, not only in relation to labor, but also in relation to environmentalists and consumers.

Postwar Animation and Postwar Blues

We have previously seen that, on the whole, the advanced capitalist economies have performed quite well during the postwar period. However, the record of these economies up to the late 1960s was decidedly superior to their achievements since that period. During the decade of the 1970s and into the early years of the 1980s, the capitalist machine has sputtered and slowed its former pace. Since the late 1960s, the rate of output growth throughout the capitalist world has fallen substantially below the levels of the first two decades of the postwar period. This is true of all the leading capitalist countries—the United States, Great Britain, France, Japan, West Germany, Italy, and Canada. Moreover, unemployment has risen sharply throughout the capitalist world, reaching more than 30 million in the early 1980s within the twenty-four member countries of the Organization for Economic Cooperation and Development (OECD). In 1982 these unemployed workers represented 8 percent of the labor force of these capitalist countries, and persistent inflation has accompanied the high unemployment in almost all of them.

Table 5-2: Key Economic Indicators of the U.S. Economy, 1947–81

	Average Annual Rates of Growth	
	1947–69	1970–81
Real corporate profits before tax[a]	3.5	−0.6
Real gross private domestic investment	4.2	1.8
Industrial production index	4.8	2.6
Real gross national product	3.9	2.8
Rate of unemployment[b]	4.6	6.4
Consumer price index	2.3	7.9
NYSE composite index[c]	9.5	2.6

[a] Adjusted for inventory valuation and capital consumption allowances
[b] Averages of annual data; these figures are not growth rates
[c] Averages of daily closing prices, from 1949 through 1981

Sources: *Economic Report of the President*, 1982, and *Federal Reserve Bulletin*, August 1982.

The Postwar Record of the U.S. Economy

Although rates of growth, unemployment, and inflation differ among the capitalist countries, the postwar record of the United States will serve as a fairly good representation of the performance of the group. Table 5-2 above divides the postwar years into two parts: the period 1947 through 1969 and the twelve-year period 1970 through 1981. The data record average annual rates of growth in each period for a number of key economic indicators. Thus real corporate profits (after inflation is removed and before tax) rose at the annual rate of 3.5 percent in the first period but actually fell in the later period at an annual rate of 0.6 percent. Real gross investment expenditures were much more buoyant in the first than in the second period. The same is true of industrial production and the real gross national product. Moreover, the annual rate of unemployment averaged only 4.6 percent from 1947 through 1969, but between 1970 and 1981 it rose to 6.4 percent. The inflation rate, as measured by the consumer price index, was only 2.3 percent in the earlier period and then climbed to 7.9 percent, on average, in the later one. Finally, the stock market, as indicated by the New York Stock Exchange's composite index (which includes all stock issues), was quite lively through 1969 but sluggish thereafter, through 1981.

Profits, Capital Formation, and Growth

The indicators in Table 5-2 are arranged, from top to bottom, so as to suggest causal relationships. In capitalist economies, the large privately owned corporations in industry, commerce, finance, and other important sectors are the central core of the growth process. If their profits are high, and promise to be even higher in the future, corporate capital formation in new plant and equipment will be large. These enlarged expenditures will increase aggregate demand for goods and services and at the same time will increase the capacity of the economy to produce the goods and services so demanded. The enlarged capital formation, therefore, leads to higher rates of growth of both industry and gross national product and to lower levels of unemployment as idle workers are absorbed into new jobs. Inasmuch as stock market investors are likely to anticipate these favorable trends, stock prices will rise to reflect the higher expected profits of corporations and the ensuing economic prosperity. (Inflation is a separate matter and will be dealt with in the section that follows.) The rising stock prices will in turn stimulate capital formation by making it easier and less costly for those corporations without ready cash to sell equities and so raise funds for their capital projects. Thus, boom conditions are produced, and they flow originally from the rising profits of the corporations.

All of these events may occur in reverse: falling profits, lower capital investments, slower industrial and overall economic growth, more unemployment, and a depressed and falling stock market.

The first series of events broadly describes the performance of the U.S. economy from 1947 to 1969. The second series of events depicts the sluggishness that in general characterized the economy from 1970 through 1981. The most important of the key economic indicators that explains this adverse turn of events is the sharp drop in the rate of growth of corporate profits from one period to the next.

During the first two decades or so of the postwar period, U.S. corporations generally expected rising profits, and so their propensity to invest in new plant and equipment was strong. The causes of this ebullience were: (1) the long postponed and unsatisfied demands built up during the depression and war years, 1930–45, and the purchasing power in the hands of the public by 1945 to turn these pent-up demands into market transactions; (2) the growing role of government as an increasingly large purchaser of goods and services, including its large military purchases in the Korean and Vietnam wars and throughout the cold-war years, and as a stabilizer of economic activity; and (3) the establishment of American dominance in the world which offered many new opportunities for profitable investments to U.S. corporations. In West Germany, Japan, and a few other countries, a strong propensity to invest was also based on each nation's need to reconstruct a war-damaged economy. These factors, taken together, led to heartened anticipations of profits and so to an investment boom for over twenty years, interrupted only occasionally by brief downturns.

When the pent-up demands were largely satisfied, when the growth rate of government expenditures for goods and services began to decline (from an annual rate of 5.7 percent in the first period to 0.9 percent in the second), and when U.S. dominance in the world had begun to diminish, profit expectations fell and so did the pace of capital formation and of growth of the economy in general.

However, another important factor, which we have previously discussed, greatly helps to explain the decline of profits of U.S. corporations during the latter part of the postwar period. That factor is the increasing strength of the critics, competitors, and foes of the capital-owning class: including global Marxism, the working classes, consumer-interest groups, environmentalists, antinuclear-energy groups, others who oppose unusually large profits made, for example, by oil companies and producers of military weapons, and still others who believe that the foreign investments of corporations are a form of neocolonialism.

U.S. corporations have also been under increasing pressure from their competitors in West Germany and Japan, and have more recently begun to feel the competition from Brazil, South Korea, and a few other rapidly developing countries. In addition, the U.S. and other capitalist economies have suffered since 1973 from the actions of the OPEC cartel, which has raised the barrel price of OPEC oil more than tenfold in less than a decade. These economies have also had some of their trade and foreign investment policies vigorously contested by alliances of underdeveloped nations. The major industrial countries, and the capital owners and managers within them, have been increasingly constrained at home and abroad in pursuing activities that would lead to greater control of world resources and to more profits.

During the latter postwar period (1970–81), these forces have joined the other factors contributing to the declining rates of profits of the corporate sector. The conjunction of these adverse influences occurred just as the Vietnam War had begun to weaken America's command over world capitalism. The lessons of that war, which were quickly becoming clear, were that America could not prevent the further spread of communism and its government could not command the allegiance of its own people in the endeavor. It was obvious by the early 1970s that the leader of the free world had its hands tied behind its back by war losses and adverse public response to them.

The period 1968–73 was the crucial one in this regard. It was during these years that the tide began to turn against the U.S. economy, and against the owners of capital in particular, as profit making came under pressure and America's allies and friends kept their distance a bit in order to pursue more independent foreign policies. It was at the end of this period that the OPEC cartel found its own forces strong relative to the declining ones of the United States.

Many of these unfavorable trends against U.S. capitalism have also adversely affected other advanced capitalist countries. They, too, have been hit by soaring oil prices, and their capital owners have also been assaulted from all sides by adversaries and competitors. The consequence is that, since the early 1970s, profits have dwindled throughout most of the capitalist world, and capital formation and economic growth have suffered as a result. Meanwhile, unemployment and unused capacity of capital goods have risen to unusually high levels during the severe recessions in 1973–75 and the early 1980s. As economies lose steam, their recessions become more frequent and their recoveries become more anemic.

Inflation

Inflation has been another economic illness of the advanced capitalist societies since the early 1970s. The combination of slow economic growth and inflation is commonly called "stagflation," a condition that has marked most capitalist societies in recent years. Inflation is a persistent rise of prices in general. It comes about when aggregate demand for goods and services exceeds the amount that producers of these goods and services wish to supply at the prevailing price levels. The excess demand may occur because demands rise beyond the current supplies, which is "demand-pull" inflation, or because supplies fall below existing demands, which is "cost-push" or "cartel" inflation.

In cost-push inflation, producers reduce supplies of goods and services at each general price level because their unit costs have risen. This is equivalent to saying that they offer the same supplies at higher prices. In this way, they pass as much of their higher costs as they can on to consumers. Rising unit costs may be caused by higher prices of raw materials, labor, energy, and other inputs, or by declines in the productivities of constant-priced inputs. In the latter case, for example, labor, receiving the same hourly compensation, may produce less per hour, thus raising unit costs of production.

In cartel inflation, producers reduce supplies because they have eliminated much competition among themselves and so, controlling the output, they are able to raise prices above competitive levels. If this process is a continuing one, persistent price increases will occur. Such price increases are the mark of inflation.

Slower output growth is not likely to accompany demand-pull inflation. The reason is that the growth of demands beyond existing supplies will induce greater production of goods and services and more employment of labor. If the growth of demands is brisk enough, the rise of employed workers will exceed the numbers being added to the labor force, with the result that unemployment will decline. Demand-pull inflation, therefore, seldom leads to stagflation.

Both cost-push and cartel inflations involve reductions of supplies below current demands, and so they are accompanied by declines of output and employment. When excess demand occurs because of falling supplies, therefore, both inflation and slower output growth are the outcomes, and the economy lapses into stagflation, with rising levels of unemployment.

A combination of cost-push, cartel, and demand-pull forces can also produce stagflation. The simultaneous occurrence of falling supplies (because, let us say, of rising unit costs) and rising demands will raise prices on both counts, as suppliers will insist on higher prices and demanders will agree to pay them. But if rising demands are not vigorous enough, output of goods and services will rise very slowly—or even fall—and, if additions to the labor supply are sizable, unemployment will grow. This combination of forces, therefore, will produce price inflation, slower output growth, and rising joblessness.

For much of the 1970s and early 1980s, the United States and other leading capitalist countries suffered from the above combination of forces. In the United States, persistent and significant price rises began in the late 1960s, when demands rose above existing supplies owing to the failure of the Johnson administration to seek tax increases to cover the rising Vietnam War expenditures. This failure reflected the administration's realization that tax increases were not possible owing to the growing opposition among the public to the war itself. Thus, serious U.S. inflation commenced with a social conflict that compelled the government to bid for its war needs against other participants in the economy seeking funds (for capital formation, housing, etc.). The results were a demand-pull inflation and rapid growth in output and employment.

However, excess demands soon developed in new forms as labor and some raw material unit costs rose sharply, so that supplies began to fall below existing demands. The subsequent quadrupling of energy prices in 1973–74 added to the supply shortages and so to excess demands. Moreover, the OPEC energy-cartel inflation fed a cost-push inflation, as the higher energy prices worked their way through the economy, resulting in higher unit costs of producing a vast number of goods and services. These combinations, in varying degrees, appeared in other capitalist countries as well.

What factors account for the excess demands—for the rise in demands above existing supplies or for the decline of supplies below current demands? What, in other words, are the root causes of the inflation that has swept so forcefully through most of the capitalist countries since the early 1970s?

Fundamentally, inflation is the result of the fragmentation of domestic and international society into increasingly numerous economic and political power centers, and the increasing friction among the centers. The

Labor Day parade in New York, 1982. (Levick—Black Star)

economic power centers, which operate primarily through economic markets, include business enterprises, farm organizations, labor unions, the oil and other cartels and marketing agreements, national governments and regions that own and control their own resources, consumer-interest groups, and environmentalist associations that limit uses of land and other natural resources. Consumer-interest groups have been concerned with the supply of shoddy products, which they have attempted to reduce, thus raising the costs to others of producing goods of higher quality. Similarly, environmentalists have tried, for example, to reduce supplies of "dirty" air and water, thereby raising costs of producing cleaner air and water. The other economic power centers have sought greater control over whatever they supply in order to sell at higher prices and so obtain larger shares of national or world income. Each power center has vied against the others for a larger share of the income pie, and by so doing each has raised costs to the others, who have retaliated by raising prices on their own controlled supplies. Continuing cost-push inflation has been the consequence of these contests among competing power centers manifested through domestic and international markets.

The political power centers comprise organizations of women, blacks, the aged, ethnic groups, the disabled, and other groups that seek to achieve gains through political, rather than economic institutions—for example, by lobbying in the national and state capitols for more government aid in one form or another. The growing number and strength of political power centers have led to so many demands on public agencies that government expenditures have outpaced tax revenues. Most of the demands have involved income maintenance, welfare, and health programs—the so-called entitlements—which have grown far beyond the public's willingness to finance them. The resulting budget deficits have generated rising demands for goods and services that have climbed far above supplies, leading, through demand-pull forces, to persistent price increases.

Inflation reflects the struggles that take place through government budgets, economic markets, and, especially, monetary institutions. Government budgets move increasingly to the deficit side as power centers demand more expenditures and all factions resist additional taxation. Monetary systems create more money in response to insistent demands by governments, businesses, consumers, and others for additional credit to restore, maintain, or increase their shares of national and world incomes. Through economic markets, power centers limit the supplies of their goods and services in order to achieve higher prices through a more favorable balance between supply and demand forces. Other economic power centers limit others' supplies and, by so doing, impose higher costs on them. Thus, inflation is fed from all sides, as society breaks up into contending groups, each looking out primarily for itself. At its core, inflation reflects the loss of shared values, or of strong leaders and willing followers, or of feelings of "community"—in short, of social cohesion achieved by whatever means. Inflation is disunity—translated through the economic system.

Stagflation

We have previously observed that the profits of U.S. corporations (as well as those of corporations in other capitalist countries) have been constrained in recent years by the growing strength of the adversaries and competitors of owners of capital. Many of these foes are the economic power centers just discussed, but they also include, as we have seen, the global spread of communism, which in various ways has reduced profit-making opportunities in much of the world for the owners of capital. In addition, the proliferation of political power centers, by raising the expenditures of governments, has led to higher (though insufficient) taxes generally, including those imposed on income from capital, thereby reducing the ability of capital owners to retain whatever profits they are able to extract from their operations.

Thus, the very same forces that lie at the heart of the inflationary process—the decline of social cohesion—also account for the lessened ability of capitalist classes to gain profits and so for the decline in the rate of capital formation and economic growth. Slower economic growth and inflation have the same basic causes—the fragmentation of society into contending groups (inflation) and the increasing strength of the contenders against owners of capital (slower growth). In brief, stagflation reflects social disunity and the relative loss of power of that society's leading class—the managers and owners of capital.

Strengths, Weaknesses, and Cures

Capitalism, like communism, has many faces. We can view capitalism's muscles from one position, its faltering pace from another. If we seek cures for the faltering pace, it would be wise to choose those that might build on the system's inherent strengths.

Strengths and Weaknesses

Capitalism's strength lies in the combination of its economic markets through which individual initiative is exerted and individual choices are made, its democratic political institutions through which voices of agreement and dissent are registered, and its social programs which guarantee at least minimal standards of living to most citizens. Over the years, the relative emphases on these elements have changed. Social programs, for example, have become more important in recent times, and economic markets have become more controlled. At times, each of these elements has complemented the others, but at other times conflicts have arisen—for instance, when social programs have reduced individual incentives to work or save. On the whole, however, capitalist societies have been able to reinforce, enlarge or diminish, or reshape one or more of the elements when such dissonance was evident—as in the 1930s when economic markets broke down, political institutions were under attack, and social programs were quite inadequate.

Capitalism's weakness lies largely in the disunity of its parts. In economics, these divisions lead to continuing conflicts over who gets what out of the income pie. Recently, these battles have been resolved by the process of inflation, which gives to some and takes from others on the basis of market power or the lack of it. In these struggles, owners of capital have lost ground to their opponents. At the same time, the advanced capitalist countries together have yielded much ground in their continuing contests with global Marxism and other anticapitalist forces. These losses at home and abroad have weakened owners of capital and have brought on lower rates of capital formation and economic growth. Stagflation—slow growth and rapid inflation—reflects some underlying debilities of capitalist societies.

Cures

The previous analysis suggests that the basic cures for stagflation are the strengthening of owners and managers of capital relative to their opponents, a greater degree of consensus among all groups in the country behind the capitalist mission of profit making and capital formation, and the reinforcement of world capitalism relative to communism. If most advanced capitalist countries pursue similar policies, the odds of defeating stagflation throughout the capitalist world become more favorable. And the elimination of stagflation might open the way for another period of vigorous economic growth unmarred by inflationary excesses. However, this scenario is more easily perceived than achieved.

The first part of the program can be advanced by a sizable redistribution of income to business corporations and the owners of capital generally from other groups in the economy. Such income shifts can be achieved by a reduction of taxes on corporations, on capital gains, and on risk taking in general; by an easing of environmental, consumer-oriented, and other regulations on business enterprises; by constraints on rising labor costs; and, broadly speaking, by policies that provide new profit-making opportunities to owners and managers of capital.

The second part of the program is even more difficult to implement. It calls for: appeals for the unification of the country; propagation of capitalism's basic message that owners and managers of capital create the conditions of prosperity, including more jobs, when they earn greater profits and reinvest them; the fashioning of national goals that have wide appeal;

and anticommunist campaigns that elicit nationalistic responses. This part of the program calls for a renewal of social cohesion, a general consensus regarding the country's goals and the means of achieving them.

The third part of the program can be promoted by: a stepped-up propaganda effort against communism and for capitalism, directed to peoples in both the Second and Third worlds; further efforts to support those governments in the Third World that oppose communism and favor capitalism; and a military buildup that includes enlarged forces to protect capitalism's vital interests in the world, to fight regional communist movements, and to supply military arms to friendly governments.

In short, stronger capitalist classes, more unity among various groups behind them, and the weakening of world communism—these are the fundamental ingredients for the renewed strength of capitalism, for the resumption of long-term capitalist growth without inflation. These are the basic ingredients for revitalizing capitalist societies.

The Reagan administration, viewing correctly the basic causes of the U.S. economy's problems, has moved in the above directions in attempts to remedy the ills. But the administration's chosen cures have, thus far, been much less successful than its analysis of the underlying difficulties.

Lesser programs are available for more modest results. Even if little is done to reduce social disunity, much can be done to reduce its impact on government expenditures and money supplies. Restraint in these financial areas can lower inflationary pressures by reducing overall demands for goods and services. Such lowered aggregate demands, however, will reduce not only inflation but the rate of output growth and the level of employment as well.

If, by contrast, policies of financial expansion are implemented to encourage economic growth and employment, inflation is likely to become more severe. These policies of financial restraint and financial expansion, therefore, lead to an improvement in one area only at the cost of worsening the other: That is to say, the management of aggregate demands leads to the unsatisfactory choices of more growth and more inflation or less inflation and less growth.

This dilemma can be at least partially overcome if policies are pursued not to raise or lower aggregate demands (by fiscal and monetary policies), but to raise aggregate supplies of goods and services. Supplies can be increased if people are induced to trade leisure for work, lazy work for hard work, consumption for saving and capital formation, and safe monetary havens for risk-taking capital ventures. The reduction and restructuring of taxes, the removal of government regulations on private enterprise, and the reconstruction of government welfare systems are among the programs that can be employed for these purposes. If such programs are successful, the output of goods and services will grow and inflation rates will decline under the weight of expanding supplies of commodities.

Although these supply-side programs do not add much strength to owners of capital vis-à-vis their opponents, do not mend the disunity of society, and do not directly promote the cause of capitalism in its global contest with communism, they nevertheless serve the purpose of moderating stagflation and, thus, of making capitalism work better in the advanced areas. Anything that makes capitalism work better at home would give it an added edge in the Third World against communism.

Thus, programs to revivify capitalism are conceivable and some significant portions of them appear to be achievable. One of capitalism's abiding strengths, as noted, has been its ability to adapt to changing conditions, and for capitalism to ferret out new combinations of policies to cure its ills is an important illustration of this adaptability. Moreover, capitalism has always utilized the business recession for the purpose of creating the conditions for another capital boom. Undoubtedly capitalism possesses the spark that will continue to ignite periods of prosperity. But these prosperities will, with equal certainty, continue to be followed by slumps.

The cycles will go on. It is likely, however, that in the future capitalism's basic weaknesses, as discussed in this chapter, will cause more frequent and severer downturns and more anemic upturns—unless capital owners throughout much of the capitalist world make a dramatic comeback with the aid of government policies that sharply raise their profit prospects and with the acquiescence of opposing groups.

Marxists have long argued that capitalism is prone both to business cycles in the short run and stagnation in the long run. Now that the special factors favoring rapid growth, which grew out of World War II, have spent themselves, the tendency for capitalism to stagnate—and "inflate"—is more pronounced than before. The capitalist system still has great strength, but much of this strength may have been gathered in the past. We may be viewing the dissipation of that legacy today. We are certainly viewing a decline in capitalism's vital powers. What we do not know is whether capitalism, in addition to producing antidotes against the Marxist poison, can also bring forth yet another elixir for itself.

A huge crowd of women and children in a "hunger march" through main Piotrkowska street in Poland to protest the shortages and bad distribution of food and other articles in local shops, July 1981. (UPI)

6

The Waning Strength of Communism

ALTHOUGH COMMUNIST REVOLUTIONS FAILED in Western Europe and America, they succeeded in the less-developed areas of the world. This diffusion of Marxism around the globe has not only threatened capitalism but has contributed to the weakening of capitalism as well. Having examined these phenomena in past chapters, let us now inspect and evaluate how Marxism has fared in the less-developed areas.

Despite the fact that communism continues to show much strength in its revolutionary assaults on capitalism, it is weakening noticeably as a vehicle for socialist economic development. Communism's waning strength in these endeavors is primarily the result of the internal problems generated by communism itself; still, capitalism has played a historical role in producing the environment within which communism's problems have germinated. Capitalism has many arrows in its quiver, and they have been aimed with fair accuracy against world communism.

To arrive at the conclusion that communism is faltering in its economic tasks, we need to understand the theory and practice of socialist economic development in less-developed countries. What happens after the revolution, when the new society sets out on a path that it hopes will lead to socialism? The section that follows addresses that question. We shall then be in a position to see why communism is beset with so many difficulties in economic development and why it is foundering in its search for sustainable socialist societies.

The Starting Point: Poverty to Socialism

If Marx and Engels Had Been Right

If Marx's and Engels' prediction that the first proletarian revolutions would occur in the most advanced capitalist countries had been correct, the working classes would have been faced with the relatively easy task of going from capitalist affluence to socialist societies containing possibly even greater wealth. In this event, the problem of achieving increased production would not have been difficult. Even the task of transforming capitalist institutions into socialist ones would have been tractable inasmuch as the enterprises constituting the heart of capitalism would have been huge and few in number, and the workers, producing in large human assemblies, would have been able to hire competent managers from their own ranks. In these circumstances, private ownership would have given way to social ownership without much friction. Similarly, central planning would have been established on the excellent foundations of microplanning by the large capitalist enterprises and macroplanning by the capitalist state.

Marx and Engels also confidently anticipated that the advanced capitalist countries, by the time of the proletarian revolutions against them, would have developed to the fullest extent their democratic institutions. The proletariat, therefore, would have had the relatively easy task of extending the democracy of the capital-owning minority into a democracy of the proletarian majority. Presumably, proletarian democracy would have permitted the working classes to control directly, through majority choices expressed democratically, the movement of their society, both in its political and economic (work) spheres. At the same time, Marx and Engels fully expected the proletarian majority to exercise a dictatorship over the dispossessed capital-owning minority who would be struggling to regain everything that they had lost. Eventually, in the future classless society of communism, democracy would become all-embracing.

Thus, if Marx and Engels had been right, the socialism that we looked at in Chapter 2 would have been formed on the foundations of advanced capitalism: a socialism in which it is more likely that the workers exercise political power democratically among themselves, the means of production are socially owned and democratically managed, appropriate planning structures replace much of the interplay of individual decision making through markets, much economic and social equality is achieved, and high and rising living standards prevail.

Two Conflicting Paths

But this was not to be. Since the proletarian revolutions occurred in the less-developed areas, the working classes were required to travel not from material affluence to socialism, but from poverty to socialism. The latter route is the vastly more difficult one because it splits into two potentially conflicting paths that confront an impoverished society: (1) a path from poverty to material wealth and (2) a path from capitalist (or presocialist) institutions and practices to socialist ones.

Path 1: from poverty to material wealth. This first path has been traversed already by the peoples of the advanced capitalist countries. Their experiences indicate that a nation can attain material wealth if individuals acquire the freedom to profit from their own efforts: in working, saving, and investing; in buying and selling; in taking risks, and the like. Their experiences also indicate that people must be able to pursue their economic interests through markets that accurately register the results of the interplay of buyers and sellers, and that society should not interfere unduly with the resulting wealth acquired by some though it should be concerned about the poverty generated by the same competitive forces. The key to success, history seems to be saying, lies in the economic freedom of individuals to do well, a drive that they exercise through competitive markets in their pursuit of personal enrichment, and in social programs to correct the worst aspects of poverty.

A young Marxist country, in considering this path after a successful revolution, would have socialized its means of production and acquired political power for its working classes. But could it retain these basic socialist elements while accepting at the same time the capitalist features of the already successful societies? This first path of development could well lead, not to socialism, but to capitalism—with the working classes ultimately losing their tenuous hold on political power to a revitalized capitalist class.

Path 2: from capitalist (or presocialist) institutions and practices to socialist ones. This second path, by contrast, requires that the young Marxist country turn away from the competitive individualism and market processes of the first path in favor of central planning, collective behavior, socialist incentives, and more equality among people in the outcomes of their endeavors. The pursuit of these socialist goals, together with social ownership of productive facilities and the political dominance of the working class, obviously lead toward a socialist society.

Young Marxist countries have generally been unwilling at the outset to attempt to attain higher living standards solely with what they consider to be capitalist values, incentives, and institutions. Instead, they have chosen to play down, but not entirely discard, the historical experience of capitalism, in the interest of promoting socialist values of cooperation; socialist incentives that stress hard and well-performed work for the sake of helping others, the revolution, the nation, or the international proletariat; and socialist planning to minimize what they regard as socially destructive and anarchic individualism in competitive and speculative markets. Nevertheless, in practice the communist countries have employed both capitalist and socialist values and incentives in striving for higher living standards, sometimes emphasizing the first and at other times the second. The tension between the two has always been great.

The attempt by less-developed Marxist countries to achieve material improvement through socialist values, incentives, and institutions (central planning) has encountered many difficulties. Collective values and incentives are compatible with a work force that has long been in collective situations—that is, in large industrial assemblies of workers that facilitate the ability of each individual to see that his problems are similar to those of his co-workers and that the solutions to these common problems lie in solidarity, in collective action. An orthodox Marxist view is that it is not possible for working classes—and especially for peasants—who have not experienced the full development of capitalism's socializing lessons, to acquire collectivist attitudes. They would be expected, instead, to be concerned with bread and butter issues and with their own personal problems and welfare. Thus, the immature working classes found in the less-developed countries still need market incentives and values, some Marxists believe, to spur them on to greater productive efforts.

The attempt by young communist countries to supplant market processes by central planning also runs into difficulties in underdeveloped settings, according to orthodox Marxism. Central planning, too, requires collectivist values, for it is a cooperative effort that contrasts markedly with the free interplay of individual decisions in economic markets. If workers and others lack collectivist values—because their working conditions are not conducive to their acquisition—they will not be prepared for successful planning. Instead of cooperation and sharing, they will look upon competition and "keeping" as the norm.

The dilemma. When developing communist countries do adopt capitalist features in order to elicit greater work effort and economic efficiency, they run the risk that such practices will prove incompatible with the social ownership of the means of production and with workers' political power. The risk, then, is that, for the sake of greater production, socialism becomes unattainable.

As previously noted, Marx and Engels thought that capitalist societies would have fully developed "bourgeois" democratic institutions awaiting the victory of the revolutionary proletariat, who could then build on them. Since these revolutions, however, occurred in countries having few if any democratic traditions, socialist societies had to be constructed on autocratic, despotic, or centralized-feudal foundations, and Marxist socialism has embodied these oppressive political forms instead of democratic ones.

In order to carry out revolutions in these underdeveloped areas, Marxists established vanguard communist parties apart from the workers which were intended to lead the workers to socialist revolutions. Lenin argued that open, democratic Marxist parties would be swept away by tsarist spies and police. He therefore demanded the formation of a close-knit, secret, professional party comprising intellectuals who had an understanding of socialism, which they would impart to a working class that itself had a natural interest primarily in wages and conditions of work.

Thus, the lack of democratic institutions in these countries was almost perfectly reflected in their absence within the Marxist working-class movements. The communist parties that led the working classes to victorious revolutions continued to exercise their leadership and control over the workers after the revolution and during socialist economic development. Party and workers, therefore, became separate bodies, the former always dominant, the latter always subordinate. The workers were denied direct access to the controls of state and society.

The subordination of workers to the party was caused not only by the circumstances demanding a powerful party, but also by the frailty of the working classes in the areas of the world where Marxism triumphed. In these less-developed countries, the production processes had not prepared the working classes for leadership. The workers were preoccupied with economic survival and disorganized owing to the predominance of small-scale production and agriculture—which put them in limited groups more or less isolated from one another and prevented them from becoming aware of themselves as a class. The workers were also heavily burdened with feudal views that comprised relationships of superiority and inferiority, the importance of saviors, and the unquestioned good will of the workers' political leaders. In addition, the levels of culture, literacy, and education of the workers were low.

Thus, in the absence of workers well-prepared for leadership of the new society, a bureaucracy—the party and government functionaries—took command. For precisely the same reason that a vanguard communist party was needed to fulfill the revolution, a party-state bureaucracy was required to lead the country, after the revolution, toward socialism. These bureaucracies may or may not represent principally the interests of the working classes—instead of their own interests—but in either event the bureaucracies rule and the workers work. The East German Marxist Rudolf Bahro wrote in *The Alternative in Eastern Europe* (1978) that the former leader of Poland's Communist party, Edward Gierek, told the workers after the December 1970 uprising: "You work well, and we will govern well"! Is there a clearer admission than that of the chasm between party and workers?

All communist nations today have such bureaucracies. Most of them are led by civilians but some, at times, are headed by the military—as in Poland in 1982 and China during a few years of the Cultural Revolution in the late 1960s. (But the military is much less prominent in politics in the communist countries than it is in the underdeveloped capitalist world.) Not only do the bureaucracies exist throughout the communist world, but, as Bahro wrote (though with irony): "There is no field in which [these societies have] made greater progress than in the breadth, depth, and diversity of the bureaucratization process."

The expanding party-state bureaucracies, by their very nature, tilt the balance toward central planning, tight controls, and collectivist incentives and away from economic freedoms exercised through market processes for both workers and managers. As a consequence, the historical forces that led to the dominance of the party have also contributed to the decision regarding whether the path to greater production (path 1) should be pursued with the aid of capitalist or socialist values, incentives, and institutions—or with what mixture of the two.

The basic dilemma facing the young Marxist countries is that the use of socialist elements is not enduringly successful in eliciting hard work from the workers and economic efficiency from the system, but the use of capitalist elements, which yield larger production gains, undermines the socialist foundations of the new society. China, several Eastern European countries, and Cuba have experimented—and are still experimenting—with various mixtures of capitalist and socialist elements in the attempt to find a combination that will contribute to higher living standards and to a socialist society. So far such a combination has not been achieved.

Alternative Strategies to Attain Socialism

To this point, we have discussed only part of the problem facing young Marxist countries—whether to use capitalist or socialist values, incentives, and institutions in pursuing path 1 to higher levels of production. However, inasmuch as socialism is the attainment of both higher living standards and socialist institutions and practices (including the socialist values and incentives discussed above), both paths 1 and 2 must be followed to attain this new society. Hence, another problem involves the choice of whether at first to build up the country's productive capacity (to attain higher living standards) and later transform the presocialist institutions and practices into socialist ones, or to reverse this order.

A strategy for reaching socialism is a decision to combine, over time, paths 1 and 2 in certain ways. Should the productive capabilities of the country be greatly expanded *before* most of the socialist institutions and practices are established? (The workers, however, must possess political control of the state from the beginning, even if only indirectly and tenuously through the communist party. Otherwise, as Marxists reason, socialism cannot be achieved.) Or should these institutions and practices be formed first as the basis for later gains of production? Can the two tasks be carried out at the same time?

This problem is illustrated in the diagram on the next page. In this drawing the productive capabilities of a young Marxist country (such as Angola or Mozambique), as measured by its national income per capita,

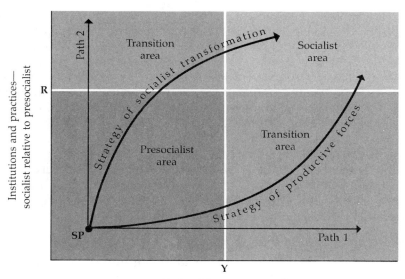

National income per capita
(the productive forces)

are shown along the horizontal axis. The extent to which socialist institutions and practices have replaced the presocialist ones (most likely tribal, feudal, and capitalist) is recorded along the vertical axis. Because revolutionary Marxism was driven out of the advanced centers of capitalism into the less-developed areas, the communist party in a poor country must seek a strategy for the attainment of socialism from the starting point (*SP*) of a very low income per capita and with few elements of socialism in place.

In the diagram, we assume that the socialist requirement of "higher living standards" is met when the less-developed country's income per capita reaches *Y* on the horizontal axis. We further suppose that the requirement that higher living standards must be attained "within the framework of socialist institutions" is met when the country reaches *R* on the vertical axis. Inasmuch as both requirements are necessary for the attainment of socialism, the socialist area in the drawing lies above and beyond the presocialist area. (In the same way, the area of communism would lie above and beyond the socialist area, starting at much higher levels of *Y* and *R*.) Also shown in the diagram are path 1, which leads from poverty to wealth, and path 2, which involves the transformation of presocialist institutions and practices into socialist ones. Neither path alone can reach the socialist area; for that, a strategy combining the two paths is required.

Starting from *SP,* a young Marxist country can seek to establish a socialist society by following either of the two main strategies, or some combination of them. If it chooses the strategy of raising productive forces, the country builds up its productive capabilities for some time before it begins to establish socialist institutions and practices to replace the presocialist ones— for example, collective farming to replace private farming, nationalized industries to eliminate private-enterprise ones, and socialist incentives to minimize capitalist motivations and values. This strategy leads through a transition area that meets one of socialism's requirements (increasing the level of income per capita) but not the other (attaining socialist institutions and practices).

If the country chooses the strategy of socialist transformation, it first establishes most of the elements of socialism before making a substantial effort to increase its production. This strategy also leads through a transition area, in which socialist institutions and practices are in place but the young Marxist nation is still too poor to warrant calling it a socialist society.

Strategy of Raising Productive Forces

The reason a communist party might choose the strategy of building its productive forces—which approximates the strategy favored by Lenin for the Soviet Union and by Liu Shao-ch'i for China—is the belief that socialist institutions and practices are unsustainable if they are not supported by higher levels of production. For instance, it may be thought that successful collective farms require appropriate farm machinery, power generation, chemical fertilizers, and other complementary modern inputs, which only a productive economy can supply. In the absence of these factors of production, the output of collective farms would be low and thus disappointing to their members, who would then have pressing incentives to supplement their incomes through private activities. Thus, the collective farms would be undermined and eventually would languish. Consequently, some Marxists argue, it is necessary for a country to achieve high production levels before it undertakes to "socialize" the economy in any substantial way.

The opponents of this strategy included Stalin, Mao, and to some extent Trotsky. They and others alleged that, when the party retains many of the country's feudal and capitalist institutions and practices in the one-sided interest of raising the productive capabilities of the economy, it runs the very high risk that the capitalist mode of production and its values will win out over socialism in the end. This is because the party will use capitalist incentives and values to spur on the workers, the profit motive to energize the managers of enterprises, and the interplay of individual decision making through markets. Such policies, it is claimed, will lead to selfish behavior, materialism, speculation, gross income inequalities, and the reemergence of the capital-owning class that prospers from these capitalist institutions and practices. Hence, the opponents of this strategy have urged its abandonment in favor of one that does not have to rely so heavily on "the enemy's" strong points.

Strategy of Socialist Transformation

The rationale behind the strategy of socialist transformation (traced out by the upper curve in the diagram) is that the immediate establishment of socialist institutions and practices is necessary to eliminate the presocialist forms that supported the privileged positions of the old ruling classes—and thus to get rid of the old ruling classes themselves—and to release the oppression exerted on the working classes by these feudal and capitalist forms. Some Marxists, especially Mao, have argued that, once the party eliminates the burdensome presocialist institutions and practices, the energies and abilities of the masses of workers will be released and production will soar. When workers become the masters of society and are supported by socialist customs, their passivity and slothful ways, which they acquired in their former subordinate positions, will disappear, to be replaced by much vitality and displays of hitherto hidden talents. Consequently, Mao and others have alleged, production gains can eventually be enormous by following this strategy, and the restoration of capitalism will be a much lesser danger along this route.

The opponents of this strategy, as we observed, have stated that socialist institutions are not sustainable without the basic support of a highly productive economy. They have also argued that the strategy of socialist transformation leads to such a series of radical social changes in so short a time that the resulting instability would reduce labor productivity and perhaps even seriously diminish the support of the working classes for the new regime. Workers need food in their stomachs before they need central planning, social ownership of the productive facilities, greater democracy in their work places, and collectivist attitudes.

Other Strategies

Communist parties have other strategies available to them. "Mixed strategies" employ first one and then the other of the main strategies. For example, the Communist party of the Soviet Union, headed by Stalin, inherited from Lenin a strategy similar to that of building the productive forces. Within a few years, Stalin, in effect, moved the Soviet Union up, in a giant leap, to the strategy of socialist transformation, from which point he engaged the country in a forced march to raise its production as rapidly as possible. On the other hand, some communist parties, after having followed for some years a strategy akin to that of socialist transformation, have moved down, in a sudden drop, to a new strategy that emphasizes less "socialism" and more production. This has happened throughout most of the Eastern European countries, in Cuba, in China after Mao's death in 1976, and during the mid-1960s in the Soviet Union.

A "combined strategy" pursues a single route to socialism, which is a weighted combination of the two main strategies. Instead of going all-out for a time on either production or socialist transformation, the party can try to pursue both activities simultaneously. This strategy has been advocated on the ground that the attainment of socialist institutions and practices, without the attainment as well of higher living standards, is not sustainable, and that production gains alone will lead to capitalism, not socialism. Therefore, both tasks must be accomplished together; each will support the other. Most communist countries have followed this combined strategy for short periods during the early stages of their economic development programs, for at these times it is necessary to do some "socializing" while early efforts are being made to raise production levels.

No country, however, has held to the combined strategy over any extended period, presumably because of the heavy costs of doing so. Unrelenting socialist transformations are upsetting to the economy in general, for they bring about constant change and leave nothing stable for very long, and they draw the energy and attention of great numbers of people away from other important activities, including production. Moreover, a strategy that gradually and continuously revolutionizes existing institutions and practices relinquishes the advantages associated with shorter and more concentrated efforts. One such advantage is the support that one program gives to another, when both are carried out simultaneously. For example, when a central planning structure is established and, at the same time, enterprises are nationalized, each enhances the effectiveness of the other. Central planning is more effective when there are responsive state enterprises, and the latter work better when there is a rational plan for their operations. Another advantage of concentrated, rather than gradual and piecemeal, efforts in socialist transformation is that there are often thresholds beyond which a country must go if the transformed institution or practice is to function properly. Thus, "a bit" of land reform, "a bit" of central planning, or "a bit" of workers' democracy is not likely to be effective or viable. A minimum quantum of change in each case is necessary, though not sufficient, for success.

Although there are advantages to doing several things at once within the area of socialist transformation, communist countries have found few if any advantages to carrying out, on a more or less continuous basis, both socialist transformation and programs to increase production. Instead, socialist transformations have generally come in a few bursts, with long periods of relative calm between the bursts during which production problems are paramount. This pattern has prevailed in Eastern Europe, the Soviet Union, and China.

Mao Zedong and his followers claimed that simultaneous efforts in both directions, sustained over limited periods of time, could yield enormous overall gains. Their argument was that, when people become involved in changing their institutions and practices to socialist forms, they develop at the same time their own skills and capabilities, and form clearer and more accurate perceptions of the world, thus becoming potentially more productive. And when, at the same time, people are encouraged to fulfill current plans for economic development, the resulting higher production levels provide a sounder basis on which the new socialist institutions can grow and prosper. The Chinese, under Mao, apparently had some temporary successes with such combined programs, but the current Chinese leaders have insisted that on balance these programs were decided failures, with costs that far exceeded their benefits. In any case, Mao and his followers did not urge such programs on a continuous basis but only in discontinuous waves. Hence, their arguments were meant to support the bursts of socialist transformations referred to above—accompanied by equal attention to raising production levels.

A Summary: The Fundamental Dilemmas

From a starting point of poverty, a young communist country faces a most difficult—and perhaps impossible—task in striving for both much higher living standards and a sustainable socialist society. A fundamental dilemma confronting such a country is that the active pursuit of either goal tends to endanger the attainment of the other. This is true whether the goals are pursued one at a time or simultaneously. (Only Mao's experiences of brief success with the sporadic use of the combined strategy throw some doubt on this conclusion.) Therefore, all strategies for the attainment of socialism which commence from poverty have inherent weaknesses.

A second fundamental dilemma facing a young communist country is that, while a sustainable socialism probably must have strong democratic features to elicit the continuing support of the populace, the attainment of any socialism at all in a less-developed country has required the undemocratic leadership of a dominant communist party. This requirement has grown out of the prerevolutionary conditions that called forth such a party and that caused frailty of the working classes. And the prerevolutionary conditions were principally those associated with poverty.

Hence, it is poverty that lies at the heart of both dilemmas.

Accumulating Difficulties

After a communist country chooses a strategy, or a set of strategies, leading to a socialist society, it will at some time become engaged in central planning, through enterprises that are socially owned, to achieve its goals of economic development. The developmental goals would ordinarily include certain annual rates of growth of the gross national product, a desired division of the output between consumption and capital formation, a fair distribution of the incomes arising from the production of goods and services, price stability, and adequate provision of health, education, job training, and welfare services to as many people as possible. Whatever their ideological persuasion, nation-states also want an adequate national defense system. Alongside these goals, as we have seen, is the aim of achieving a sustainable socialist society that maintains momentum toward the classless society of communism. This aim calls for, among other things, changes in people's values, incentives, and forms of behavior in keeping with socialism and the political dominance of the working classes. Have the means been adequate for achieving these ends?

The Contours of Success

It is not difficult to find a wealth of data pointing to certain economic successes of communist countries during the postwar period. A group of these countries—including the Soviet Union, all the Eastern European nations, China, and North Korea—raised their gross national product per capita at an average annual rate of somewhere between 5 and 7 percent from 1950 to 1980. According to the World Bank, this performance compares to growth rates of only 1 to 2 percent for noncommunist low-income countries and of 3.5 to 4.5 percent for both noncommunist middle-income countries and the advanced capitalist countries. (Each of these figures is an unweighted average for the particular group, not weighted by national population sizes.) At the growth rates achieved by the communist countries, incomes per capita would double about every eleven years. However, production in these countries has outrun consumption, because so much of the productive output has been used for military buildup and capital formation (buildings, factories, dams) rather than current consumption.

In these aggregate terms, the two giants in the communist group also sparkled economically. According to the World Bank and the Joint Economic Committee of the U.S. Congress, the Soviet Union's gross national product per capita grew over the thirty-year period at an average annual rate of 4 to 4.5 percent, and its industrial production index climbed in every year of that period without a single drop, at an annual rate of more than 7 percent. By contrast, the industrial production index of the United States over the same period fell six times, rising on the average by only 4 percent per annum. According to the above sources, China's postwar performance easily surpassed that of the Soviet Union in the two areas noted, except that China's industrial production index was as erratic as that of the United States. Putting quality of commodities aside for the moment, both the Soviet Union and China increased consumption of goods and services per capita at twice the postwar rate of the United States, according to data from the U.S. Central Intelligence Agency.

The relatively high growth rates achieved by the group of communist countries during the postwar years are the result of high saving and investment rates; a determined allocation of many of these resources through the planning system to the most promising growth areas, such as heavy industry and scientific and engineering research and training; rapid increases of labor supplies (surpassing population gains), as women and the underemployed and unemployed were added to the active work rolls; the transfer of workers from low productivity jobs to much higher ones—often from the rural to the urban areas; and a rise in literacy, skills, health, and general education of the population. These undertakings were facilitated by the ability of the several communist parties to mobilize the relevant people and resources—tasks that themselves were made less difficult by the presence of national planning structures and the social ownership of most of the important capital goods and other real resources.

The communist countries have not only grown rapidly, on the average, but they have had a good record of distributing the fruits of their growth in equitable ways. Income distribution is apparently more equal in the Marxist countries than in the Third World or the advanced capitalist nations. According to a study in *Redistribution with Growth* (1975, edited by Hollis Chenery), the bottom 40 percent of families receive about 25 percent of national income in the Marxist countries, roughly 16 percent in the advanced capitalist countries, and only 12 percent in the noncommunist less-developed states. Since property income is fairly large and highly concentrated in most capitalist countries, the elimination of this single factor in the communist countries accounts for much of the differences in these distributions of national income.

The Soviet Union's success in narrowing income disparities since Stalin's death in 1953 is attested to by several scholars. This income redistribution was achieved through a series of measures, extending over fifteen years. These measures raised wages of the lowest income groups (especially in the services sector), boosted the minimum-wage rate of urban workers by more than a third and of rural workers by about a half, raised by more than a third the minimum pensions of disabled workers and the minimum benefits of survivors, established a national social insurance system for peasants (similar to the one for workers), lowered taxes on low-income families, promoted greater geographical equality through state investments, and in general narrowed considerably the gap between urban and rural living standards. In the last thirty years, real disposable income per capita in the Soviet Union has grown by more than 5 percent per year—

over twice the rate in the United States—and many of these gains in the U.S.S.R. have gone to the lower income groups.

Although comparable data do not exist for China, scholars generally agree that living standards in that country, while still low, are about as uniform among the urban population (about 20 percent of total population) as can be found anywhere in the world. Among the population as a whole, few people are permitted to fall below their minimal needs and few are able to soar far above the average income. Nevertheless, urban living standards in China are still notably higher than rural living standards, and this gap may have grown during the past few decades. Moreover, rural family incomes differ markedly from one region to another—owing to differences in fertility of land and relatively low migration of people from low to high income areas.

The Soviet Union and several Eastern European countries improved the living standards of their people during the postwar years to such an extent that by 1980 they had almost reached equality with the advanced capitalist countries in many facets of health, education, and welfare, even though the communist countries have less than half the income per capita of the advanced ones. For example, according to World Bank data, life expectancy at birth in 1980 was only a few years less in Eastern Europe and the Soviet Union than it was in Western Europe, the United States, and Canada. However, a 1982 study by the Soviet expert Murray Feshbach revealed that Soviet death rates, especially for males, have risen sharply since 1964, owing largely to adverse living standards and widespread alcoholism. Although low-income countries generally have low life expectancies, communist Cuba, far behind the United States in this respect in 1960, drew even with its giant neighbor by 1980.

In recent years, the World Bank reports, the Third World countries have had on the average one physician for every several thousand people (for India, 3,600; for Indonesia, 13,600). The (unweighted) average for the advanced capitalist countries is about one physician for every 600 people, and the figure for Eastern Europe, the Soviet Union, Mongolia, China and Cuba averages about 650. The communist countries badly trailed the advanced capitalist nations in 1950 in the number of students in secondary schools as a percentage of the relevant age group. By 1980, however, many of the communist countries had caught up to the capitalist levels. China, Cuba, and Mongolia reached enrollments of between 70 percent and 80 percent of the relevant age group by 1980; India at 27 percent and Indonesia at 22 percent fairly represented the Third World countries. The communist countries considered above still lag behind the advanced capitalist nations in enrollments in higher education. Adult literacy rates have also risen sharply in Yugoslavia, China, Rumania, and Cuba, and they are now on a par throughout the Soviet bloc with those in the capitalist world.

In outlining the failures of the communist regimes, it is best to utilize the Marxist framework itself, as developed in Chapter 2. Marx and Engels postulated that a mode of production such as socialism includes the society's productive forces (land, labor, and capital goods), which reflect not only the economic power of the country but also the way in which people relate to their natural and man-made environment. The mode of production also comprises the social relations of production, which are the institutions and practices most closely associated with the way society produces, exchanges, distributes, and plans its output of goods and services. These relations of production show how people relate to each other—their class relations, in particular—in the economic realm. Finally, the mode of production is topped by the superstructure, which consists of the ideas, values, culture, and noneconomic systems of authority (political, educational, legal, military) that support the class structure of that society. Marxists often refer, in shorthand, to the superstructure as comprising the ideology and politics of society. We can now look at each of these areas in studying the failures of communism.

The forces of production. We have seen that the communist countries as a group built up and utilized their productive forces to good advantage during the postwar period as a whole. However, in general, since the mid-1970s their output growth rates have declined from their earlier levels. Moreover, a few of them, such as the Soviet Union, have had declining growth rates of output for a decade or two. Many of them have encountered their most serious problems in the agricultural area. Table 6-1 and Table 6-2 offer some relevant data from 1961 to 1979 on gross national product, and from 1966 to 1979 on industrial and agricultural production, for the Soviet Union, Eastern Europe (except Albania), China, and North Korea. Although several estimates exist for each of the three variables, since all of them reveal the imprint of declining economies from the mid-1970s or even earlier, the figures presented here may be considered typical.

The data for gross national product show that, in general, growth rates were relatively high in the first half of the 1960s, somewhat lower in the second half of that decade, but then rose in the years 1971 through 1975. Every communist country except Yugoslavia slumped in the latter half of the 1970s, although China and Rumania slipped only a little from very high levels. Notice that the Soviet Union had declining growth rates of gross national product throughout. All of these economies continued to founder into the early years of the 1980s.

The data in Table 6-2 present annual rates of growth in industrial and agricultural production for the same group of countries, but for the shorter period 1966–79. Although the growth rates of industrial production also

Table 6-1: Average Annual Growth Rates of Real GNP

	1961–65	'66–70	'71–75	'76–79
China	4.9	7.2	7.0	6.7
North Korea	9.8	5.7	10.5	2.0
USSR	5.6	5.1	3.5	3.1
Eastern Europe	4.4	4.0	4.8	3.5
Bulgaria	6.3	4.8	4.6	2.1
Czechoslovakia	2.0	3.5	3.4	2.1
East Germany	2.9	3.2	3.5	2.6
Hungary	4.2	3.1	3.3	2.5
Poland	4.1	3.8	6.4	2.7
Rumania	5.0	4.6	6.7	6.0
Yugoslavia	6.1	5.2	5.7	6.4
Averages (unweighted)	5.1	4.6	5.5	3.6

Sources: National Foreign Assessment Center, *Handbook of Economic Statistics 1980*, pp. 24, 28. Also see World Bank, *World Bank Atlas, 1976;* World Bank, *World Development Report 1978;* and World Bank, *World Development Report 1982.*

Table 6-2: Average Annual Growth Rates of:

	Industrial Production			Agricultural Production		
	1966–70	'71–75	'76–79	'66–70	'71–75	'76–79
China	9.7	9.7	7.0	4.6	3.4	3.0
North Korea	NA	NA	NA	2.1	9.0	3.4
USSR	6.3	5.9	3.5	3.8	−0.1	2.0
Eastern Europe	8.3	8.8	6.4	1.1	2.5	1.6
Bulgaria	13.0	9.5	8.6	−2.6	1.0	−2.1
Czechoslovakia	6.0	5.9	3.8	6.9	1.5	0.3
East Germany	5.8	5.8	5.0	1.0	3.2	0.5
Hungary	7.0	7.6	5.0	1.2	3.2	2.3
Poland	8.0	10.9	5.7	−1.1	1.6	1.5
Rumania	12.7	13.7	9.2	−1.2	3.6	6.7
Yugoslavia	5.4	8.1	7.3	3.2	3.2	1.8
Averages (unweighted)	8.2	8.6	6.1	1.8	3.0	1.9

Sources: Joint Economic Committee, Congress of the United States, *East European Economic Assessment*, Part 2, pp. 38–39, July 10, 1981. Joint Economic Committee, Congress of the United States, *Soviet Economy in a Time of Change*, Volume 1, October 10, 1979, p. 422. National Foreign Assessment Center, *Handbook of Economic Statistics 1980*, pp. 36, 37, 60.

declined in the second half of the 1970s, they were still remarkably high in these years by world standards. The industrial performance of the advanced capitalist countries, for example, was significantly lower during these years, and most of the Third World countries performed even more weakly.

The agricultural production figures show a mixed picture. These growth rates, like the others, declined on the average during the latter half of the 1970s, but they still remained above their levels of the previous decade. The agricultural data are also more erratic than the industrial data, which mainly reflects the greater influence of variable weather conditions on crops than on industrial processes. Moreover, the agricultural figures are substantially lower than the industrial growth rates. A principal reason for this is that agriculture, involving as it does land that is relatively fixed in supply, is more subject to diminishing returns than is industry. In addition, the communist countries in general have run into more difficulties with food production owing to adverse weather conditions and to weaknesses in the socialist organization of the agricultural sector.

The worsening economic performances of these "older" communist countries have been matched by the mounting economic problems of the newer members of the Marxist camp. Angola became a communist country in the mid-1970s. Since that time, its economy has been hurt badly not only by the past struggle for independence but also by the continuing civil war and attacks by South Africa. It has also been damaged by the fall in the prices of its three main exports—oil, diamonds, and coffee. In 1981 industrial output was well below the level of 1973, and the country was importing much of its food, having supplied 90 percent of it itself in 1974. Some of these difficulties can be traced to the economic policies of the new government, such as the policy of paying low prices to the producers of food, which has discouraged food production, and its socialization policies, which have elicited resistance from some peasants and workers. However, it should be realized, in the cases of Angola and most of the other emerging communist countries, that a large part of their difficulties come from the poor legacies they inherited from their former colonial rulers as well as from current policies.

Mozambique also joined the Marxist group in the mid-1970s, and it too, having adopted central planning and social ownership of many economic facilities, has encountered severe problems. Owing partly to droughts and to low prices paid to agricultural producers, the new government has not been able to restore the previous efficiency of this sector. The industrial sector has suffered from shortages of raw materials and managerial inefficiencies. Economist Nicos Zafiris in *The New Communist Third World* (1982), edited by the Soviet expert Peter Wiles, estimated that the people of Mozambique "are [now] much poorer and less productive than in 1973." Indeed, income per capita appears to have fallen by at least 10 to 15 percent since that year.

Ethiopia, which became a Marxist country in December 1974, has been unable since that time to increase its income per capita. It has been plagued not only by the demands on the economy of continuing warfare (the Ogaden War with Somalia and fighting against the guerrilla secessionist movement in Eritrea in the north), but also by serious droughts, pest infestations, difficulties associated with land reforms, rural cooperatives, and the nationalization of some basic industries, and declining aid from the West. Since 1974, food production per capita has fallen and manufacturing output has stagnated.

The People's Democratic Republic of Yemen (South Yemen) became a Marxist nation in the late 1960s, shortly after it gained independence from British colonial rule. The new government carried out land reforms, nationalization, and comprehensive economic planning which included a system of price controls. The World Bank estimated that the economy of South Yemen grew by the phenomenal annual rate of 12 percent during the 1970s. This record was achieved largely because of rising remittances from Yemeni workers in other oil-rich Arab countries, foreign economic assistance, and new investments in industry and other crucial areas of the economy. There have been, however, emerging problems of labor shortages, agricultural stagnation, and growing income disparities between urban and rural dwellers. But South Yemen's problems do not seem to be particularly troublesome within the context of its expanding economy.

With regard to other young communist nations, it is clear that the Socialist Republic of Vietnam, the People's Democratic Republic of Lao (Laos), and Kampuchea (Cambodia) are all struggling to get off the ground. Zimbabwe (Rhodesia), given its delicate geographical position next to South Africa and the continuing presence of many white settlers, is moving very slowly toward Marxism. Nicaragua is still in a transitional stage, and the (perhaps pseudo-) Marxist nation of the People's Republic of Benin (Dahomey) continues to be mired in terrible poverty, with virtually no growth per capita. Guinea, in west Africa, which has had a Marxist (or at least a socialist) government for some years, found its economy in a shambles by the early 1980s and so, according to the *Wall Street Journal* (September 21, 1982), began to turn away from Marxism toward private enterprise and Western aid.

The economic problems encountered by most communist countries in the late 1970s and early 1980s were caused by (1) failures of their own policies, planning programs, and socialization measures; (2) the rising prices of energy in 1973–74 and again in 1979–80; (3) the retardation of growth in the advanced capitalist countries during most of the 1970s and the early years of the 1980s; (4) the inadequate economic legacies that many of the

Female field hands, at work near the Volga River, point up a severe shortage of machinery in the farm system. (Wright—Gamma/Liaison)

young communist countries inherited from former colonial rulers; and (5) several special factors, such as the United States' continuing embargo on Cuba, China's sudden termination of aid to Albania and its invasion of Vietnam, successive years of poor weather conditions in the Soviet Union, and the persistence of warfare in Angola, Ethiopia, Kampuchea, and elsewhere.

Both internal and external factors, therefore, are responsible for the recent economic growth problems of the communist countries. In the case of the Soviet Union and some of the Eastern European countries, however, it is fairly clear that communist policies themselves were largely responsible for a major part of the economic difficulties. The mounting troubles of the Soviet Union and a few of its satellites began to appear as early as the 1960s, before the onset of the oil crisis and the retardation of growth in the capitalist economies. All of these countries were struggling in the 1960s with reforms of their economic systems, in attempts to revitalize the forces of economic growth.

There were several internal reasons for the slowing of growth in the Soviet bloc countries. First, the new supplies of capital goods, labor, and land began to contract. Many of these countries had to produce more consumption goods and services to satisfy the growing demands of the people for higher living standards as they became increasingly aware of consumption levels in the West. Rising military production in the Soviet Union also crowded out much needed investment in capital equipment and structures. By the 1960s, surplus supplies of labor and land were fast disappearing throughout the area; industry could no longer tap as freely as it once did the rural underemployed, and many women had already been drawn into the labor force. The most fertile land and the most accessible natural resources had been exploited.

Second, economic growth rates suffered because of the increasing unwillingness of the labor force to work as hard and with as much perseverance as they did in the earlier years of the new regimes. The fall in work incentives has been ascribed to the continuing and often increasing authoritarian control of people's daily lives by the communist parties, to the lack of either political or economic democracy among the working classes, to overcentralized and cumbersome planning, and to the dwindling supplies of high-quality consumer goods. The declining appeal of Marxism-Leninism as an ideology to mobilize the energies of the population also acted as a drag on diligent labor—and alcoholism acted as a drug.

Third, these countries also encountered increasing difficulties with central planning, owing to the growing number of products and to the increasing complexities of the economies, which made them more difficult to monitor. As time went on, the administered price structures became less and less appropriate to actual demand and supply conditions, which led to extensions of black markets, long queues waiting for rationed or short supplies of goods, lower qualities of goods, and general inefficiencies in the allocation of economic resources.

The Chinese economy also suffered from some of these infirmities, but in many respects it presents a different picture. The current Chinese leaders have traced China's problems of the late 1970s and early 1980s to the faulty policies sponsored by the party under Mao Zedong during the Great Leap Forward and the Cultural Revolution. Although the indictments of Mao have been exaggerated for political reasons, his policies in the late 1950s and mid-1960s did result in chaotic social and economic conditions. However, Chinese growth rates have remained very high by any standards, and these set China apart from most of the Soviet bloc countries.

Faulty central planning and unwise policies played roles of some importance in the poor growth performances of Cuba in the 1960s, Poland in the late 1970s and early 1980s, and North Korea during its six-year plan of 1971–76.

Nevertheless, these internal planning and policy weaknesses are by no means the full story of declining rates of output growth in communist countries. The "outside" factors already discussed, including soaring oil prices and the serious downturn of economic activity in the capitalist nations, contributed importantly to the growing difficulties in many of the communist countries. If one looks at the economic growth performances of the communist countries throughout the postwar period, one cannot easily dismiss the contention that these economies have had remarkably good records. By and large, the greatest weakness of communism does not lie in the area of growth but rather in its decaying social relations and tottering superstructures.

Decaying social relations and tottering superstructures. In Marx's socialist society, the social relations of production would reflect the leadership of the working classes in the economic life of the nation. This leadership would be exercised principally in the production of goods and services, in which workers and their managers would be the decision makers and in which high and rising labor productivity would prevail, motivated increasingly by collective and nonmaterial incentives. The rising volumes of goods and services would be distributed among the populace in increasingly equitable ways, and the exchanges of goods and services would be facilitated by well-functioning markets. The working classes would also take leadership in the comprehensive planning of the economy, aided by the socialist institutions of agricultural cooperatives and nationalized industries—that is, by the social ownership of the major means of production.

In the superstructure of politics, ideology, and culture, the working classes would have political control of the state and its agencies, exercising a dictatorship over the former ruling classes but extending and deepening democratic processes among themselves. The socialist ideology of cooperation and sharing, support of working-class revolutionary movements and Marxist-socialist societies around the world, and the attainment of the basic needs of the people would gain over their capitalist and feudalist counterparts. A culture that comprised the best of the past and the portrayal of the lives of the workers in the present would evolve, along with transformed institutions in education, law, the military, and other noneconomic areas of the society.

In the actual communist societies, on the other hand, the working classes are at least one step, and usually many more, removed from the power to control their own lives, whether in the areas of politics, work, planning, or most anything else. Instead, party-state bureaucracies have been imposed over the workers and peasants, denying them not only the controls of the state and society but also the right to protest the authoritarian mantles smothering them. The swelling and domineering bureaucracies have weakened the working classes in socialist societies that historically have called for the leadership of the workers—just as the capital-owning classes have been disabled by other forces in the capitalist societies that historically have demanded the leadership of those classes. Communism and capitalism both exist in a weakened state, therefore, each without the vigorous guidance of its most important class.

The stifling party-state bureaucracies in communist societies, by debilitating the working classes and their aspirations for fuller democratic representation, have filled the empty spaces with hierarchies, secret police, censors, officials, and sham organizations. As a result, the potentially rich socialist relations among workers have decayed into relations of alienation, relations between boss and worker, official and suppliant, censor and the free spirit. Socialist politics have turned into commands, socialist ideology into the morals of beating the system, and socialist culture into the white and black of labor heroes and villains, and, sub rosa, into the hard rock and stiff jeans of the West.

To sum up, communist countries have grown economically but they have not grown into sustainable socialist societies. In terms of our earlier analysis in this chapter, these countries have fairly successfully followed the strategy of building their productive forces—traced out in the graph on page 109 by the lower route to socialism—but they have failed to follow the strategy all the way into a viable socialism. What they have settled for can best be described as "nonsocialist" modes of production for the attainment of industrialization. The working classes can transform these societies into socialist ones only by carrying out revolutions against the party-state bureaucracies now ruling them.

We have already observed that the pattern of development of capitalism has played a major role in establishing the conditions in which young communist countries were forced to find their way from poverty to both material affluence and socialism. Capitalism helped to establish the rules of a game that communism had to play and could not win. Moreover, after that good start, capitalism weakened communism even more in a variety of ways, which we are now in a position to examine.

Capitalism's Antidotes to Communism in the Less-Developed Areas

In Chapter 3, we saw how advanced capitalism defeated revolutionary Marxism in Western Europe and the United States. As just noted, capitalism also has antidotes against the communist poison in the less-developed areas of the world. What are these antidotes and how strong are they?

Capitalism's Gluts and Glitter

Business cycles. We observed in the previous chapter that the capital-owning classes in the advanced capitalist countries often strengthen themselves relative to the working classes and others during recessions and depressions: Capitalism's downturns prepare the economy for booms of capital formation, which, however, later sputter and come to a halt. Business cycles are integral vehicles of economic progress in capitalist societies.

Inasmuch as the advanced capitalist countries are still the dominant economic force in the world, their periodic downturns sharply reduce their demands for the exportable products of the communist countries, which in turn causes the communist economies to suffer and their international balances of payments to worsen (as their imports exceed their exports). Prices of minerals, raw materials, and certain crops often plummet during capitalist recessions, turning some of the smaller communist economies into near-disaster areas—unless their products can be sold at higher (subsidized) prices to the larger and more-advanced communist countries—Cuban sugar to the Soviet Union, for example. In the absence of these and similar arrangements, the smaller communist countries often have to incur foreign debt to pay for their necessary imports, and in this way they mortgage much of their future.

As a consequence, the business cycles that serve such a positive function in capitalism's longer-term progress have nothing but adverse impacts on many of the communist countries, forcing them either to suffer the adversities themselves or to transfer them to other parts of the communist world. In either case, a peculiar strength of capitalism becomes a curse for communism as a mode of economic development. But, since capitalist depressions also injure Third World countries, communism as a revolutionary force gains.

High consumption levels. Industrial capitalism had a head start over communism by 150 years, and today, more than half a century after the beginnings of communist development, capitalism continues to produce goods and services, in quantities and qualities, far surpassing communism's capabilities. And, in the present age of rapid communication, everyone in the world knows about this production differential. Capitalism's glitter of automobiles, kitchen appliances, television sets, and hundreds of other attractive consumer products weakens the progress of communism in several ways.

The knowledge of these high consumption levels raises the aspirations of many poor people in the world, leading them to increase their own consumption levels—with imports of capitalist goods if necessary—to the extent that their inadequate incomes allow them. These higher consumption expenditures reduce the real resources available for capital formation and economic growth, and hence they retard progress in the less-developed areas, including many communist countries. Moreover, the temptation of poor people to import capitalist products can play havoc with the foreign balances of payments of communist and other developing nations. In addition, the glitter of capitalism's consumer goods causes much dissatisfaction among the people of communist lands with the inability of their own societies to match those displays. The much higher incomes in Western Europe and America also attract some of the best-trained people in the developing world to these richer countries, where professional opportunities are so much better.

It is largely for these reasons that many communist countries do their best to insulate their people from "the temptations of the devil." Although "open societies" often promote economic progress within their own borders, through contacts with new ideas and technology, such openness can also seriously retard progress in the ways enumerated above. That is another dilemma that capitalism has placed before its communist rivals.

Nationalism

Capitalist societies were the first mode of production to aim for modernization. Capitalism required the elimination of small feudal pockets, the dissolution of the cellular societies of medieval times. It needed freedom to buy and sell expansively. It demanded uniform regulations and procedures, a national monetary system and predictable financial markets, as well as protection of private property rights and the enforcement of contracts. It sought a nation-state to abet it internationally and to sponsor it nationally. In all these ways, capitalism courted nationalism.

National cultures arose in Europe near the close of the Middle Ages, stimulated by wars and civil conflicts, the invention of printing, and the increasing influence of commerce. National states were formed as commercial classes opposed the pope and clergy by establishing, in theory and practice, the divine rights of monarchs. The growing needs of commerce led, later, to the transfer of much power from the monarchs to the as-

CUBA SI, YANKEES NO

JULY 26th INTERNATIONAL DAY OF SOLIDARITY WITH CUBA

...GRESSIONS AND END THE BLOCKADE
...NTANAMO BASE
...71 SPY FLIGHTS

ZIMBABWE BEGINS RECONSTRUCTION

INTERNATIONAL SOLIDARITY WITH THE PEOPLE AND STUDENTS OF ANGOLA

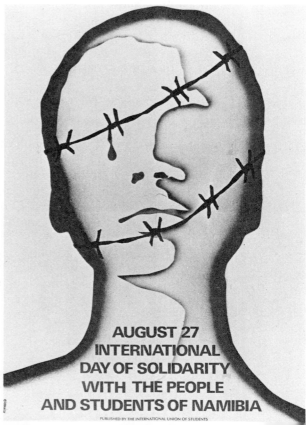

AUGUST 27
INTERNATIONAL
DAY OF SOLIDARITY
WITH THE PEOPLE
AND STUDENTS OF NAMIBIA

PUBLISHED BY THE INTERNATIONAL UNION OF STUDENTS

cending bourgeoisie. The nation-state, during the era of mercantilism (approximately 1500 to 1800), employed economic regulation to build itself into a great power, principally for the gain of the propertied interests.

However, modern nationalism first developed fully in Western Europe during the eighteenth century and especially in the revolutions and Napoleonic wars of 1789–1815. As late as 1776, in the American Declaration of Independence no appeal was made to nationalism, to "Americanism." Such pleas awaited the nineteenth century. More recently, nationalism in the less-developed areas was created out of the affronts of imperialism. Poor countries, struggling to break the bonds of colonial and feudal oppression, have embraced both revolutionary Marxism and nationalism, employing them synergistically. Once the bonds of oppression were broken, however, nationalism then went on to surpass revolutionary Marxism as the energizer for modernization. Nationalism owed its victory partly to the fact that the class conflicts incited by revolutionary Marxism ran counter to modernization's demand for heroic and joined efforts by the entire community.

Moreover, as communist countries squared off contentiously, nationalism served better than revolutionary Marxism to unite entire peoples for the defense of their countries. Marxism's divisive purposes and prophecies were dimmed before nationalism's stout appeals to solidarity in the face of danger, to the glory of the country's historical traditions, and to the beauty of her cultural accomplishments. In almost every crisis, national emotions have proven stronger and more resistant than class consciousness. Although Marxism envisages the nationalization of industries, the more dramatic event of the past few decades has been the nationalization of Marxism itself. It is this nationalization, with the consequent disunity of the world's proletariat, that has shattered the communist world into a dozen pieces, thereby weakening it as a force against world capitalism. Nationalism has been another of capitalism's weapons against its foe.

Religion

Capitalism did not invent religions but it has often countenanced them. It has felt at home with their philosophical idealism, has welcomed their diverting and often stabilizing tenors, and has favored and nurtured some at the expense of others. Religious movements, in their turn, have supported existing capitalist orders. Communism, on the other hand, has viewed all forms of religion as anathemas, while religions, on their side, have usually tried to rock the very foundations of Marxist philosophy. Generally speaking, capitalism and religions have collaborated more often than not against the heresies of worldly proletarianism.

Nevertheless, religious persuasions have at times been hostilely sighted on capitalism, too. Many Catholic convictions early opposed capitalism's excessive preoccupation with material wealth, its conviction that a man's neighbor was a customer to be gained or a rival to be overthrown. Many religious beliefs have assailed the immoderate economic rationality of capitalism. Moreover, Third World peoples have sought liberation from colonialism's lock by embracing not only revolutionary Marxism and nationalism but religious beliefs as well. In fact, the less advanced technologically such peoples have been, the more likely have they been to seek relief from their frustrations and sufferings in messianic ways, even before serious political movements were undertaken.

In the less-developed areas, advocates and followers of the world's major religions, and of the schisms within them, by warring often against each other, have further shattered the structures of proletarian internationalism. Whether religion is bellicosely communal or conciliatorily self-centered, whether it is church, sect, or mystic, it cherishes faith and undermines the credibility of a doctrine that aspires to worldwide working-class unity, collective and selfless duties, and materialist rationality. Religion threateningly confronts the messenger from a church without a heaven. Although religious beliefs can injure vital elements of capitalism, too, such as its scientific and rationalist temper, the two ideologies have considerably more in common than either has with revolutionary Marxism.

Religion is an answer to injustice, suffering, fear and terror, and death. Its appeal is to "the beyond," beyond the surface manifestations of things. Its attractions are many, quite varied, and powerful, and they rival and usually far surpass those of communism. This is important because religions and communism often attempt to appeal to the same deprived and oppressed peoples. Communism can compete up to a point, for it also satisfies a quest for community, promises solutions to earthly woes, foresees final struggles leading to a radically new society, provides chants, pilgrimages, and parades, and offers an understanding of reality. But it cannot promise an answer to death, and it denounces the deep-seated irrational temperament of the great majority of the world's people. Religion tries to overcome the despair of daily life by pointing upward to the superempirical. Marxism attempts to overcome oppression by pointing downward to the underworld of capitalist production and exploitation. Religion has the easier time of it.

In the end, capitalism, by honoring religions, has joined forces with a potent foe of communist doctrine.

Sigmund Freud (1856–1939) did not view religion in class terms or in terms of capitalism and socialism. However, he did consider religions to be illusions—that is, beliefs strongly motivated by wish-fulfillments (which may or may not be false). According to Freud, religion's tasks are to: (1) exorcize the terrors of nature; (2) reconcile men to the cruelty of fate, particularly as it is shown in death; and (3) compensate them for the sufferings and privations which a civilized life in common has imposed on them. *Civilization cannot protect individuals from the ravages of nature or from the evil designs of others or from suffering and helplessness. Religious ideas are designed to make helplessness and suffering tolerable. Freud believed that religion is comparable to a childhood neurosis. Just as many children, later as adults, surmount this, so may mankind, he thought, surmount religion after long years of further development. We will in time, Freud said, come to accept Science and discard Religion. Marxists would say that when Scientific Socialism replaces capitalism, and when socialism conquers helplessness and suffering (but not death!), religions will be discarded. (See Freud's works,* The Future of an Illusion, Totem and Taboo, *and* Civilization and Its Discontents.)

Human Rights and Democracy

Revolutionary Marxism proposes the dictatorship of the proletariat to suppress the bourgeoisie and other class enemies, and to attain, ultimately, the classless society of communism. This Marxist principle has been opposed by drives for human rights for everyone, regardless of class, and by pressures to extend political democracy. Such freedoms are the historical fruits of capitalism, now numbered among its potent anticommunist weapons. Marxists have alleged that human rights and democracy are flawed by the absence in capitalist societies of working-class political dominance: the only foundation upon which, they maintain, a true political democracy can be erected. Nevertheless, large numbers of people, in whatever political system they reside, have desperately sought to expand their freedoms—of speech, the press, assembly, due process, and religious belief. Marxism's failure to provide such expanded freedoms has been a serious blow against it.

Capitalism grew up in Western Europe under the influence of strong middle classes—the commercial, financial, and manufacturing bourgeoisie. These emerging classes insisted on freedoms for their money capital, which became concentrated in their hands through processes that, simultaneously, involved the formation of a large working class and the dissolution of monopoly and regulatory barriers to freer and expanded trade. In the early part of that era, authority shifted from the church, with its medieval ideal of a united Christendom, to the nation-state, with its political sovereignty in a fragmented secular world. The middle classes, to gain national governments, supported monarchs against the church and feudal lords, and after those struggles were largely won sought to transfer the power to themselves. The monarchs were supported against the pope and clergy by the theory of the divine right of kings and, later, by theories of national sovereignty on rational, not religious, grounds. One line of reasoning was that all civil authority was originally held by the people who had delegated it, by social contract, to the monarchs. This double-edged doctrine, when wielded by commercial classes and religious sects, led to notions of popular sovereignty. The sovereign power rested, it was argued, with the people who had the right to depose errant rulers.

Thus, the middle classes, having created the absolutist national state to counter papal dominance, now limited that state's power to intrude on private property and individual conscience. The English Bill of Rights in 1689, for example, gave political supremacy to Parliament, and stated that Englishmen possessed certain inviolable political and civil rights. The American Declaration of Independence (1776), the French Declaration of the Rights of Man and the Citizen (1789), and the first ten amendments to the U.S. Constitution (Bill of Rights, 1791), carried forward the idea of natural rights of the people—but essentially of the propertied classes, not of "the mob." The well-to-do middle classes were to be protected against both tyranny from above and runaway democracy from below.

Only in the 1800s and in this century, after long struggles by the working classes to enrich their economic and political freedoms, were democratic processes extended to them and to other groups. In much of the advanced capitalist world, these efforts have resulted in civil rights that a nation's inhabitants enjoy by law, and specified positive acts of government to protect persons against arbitrary or discriminatory treatment; in widespread political rights that extend democracy to the vast majority; and in personal freedoms that imply self-determination of the rational agent to seek individual well-being.

These freedoms have been limited in capitalist societies by the degree to which capitalism prevents some people from exercising such self-determination (including its failure to provide sufficient jobs during its periodic business downturns and its propensity to generate income inequalities), by the extent to which it appeals to an unthinking acceptance of its values, and by the extent to which capitalist societies reduce the freedoms of minorities and other disadvantaged persons to formalities. Although Marxism has advertised that it offers fuller and more genuine freedoms than capitalism provides, in practice the claim has not been achieved. Nor have Marxist freedoms appealed to the world's people to anywhere near the same degree that capitalist freedoms have. For this reason, communism has been stymied by another of capitalism's powerful weapons.

Karl Marx believed that one is not free if one acts on mere impulse or inclination. True freedom is not the freedom of caprice; it is not irrational, destructive, and meaningless responses to events and circumstances. For Marx, the freedom of individuals resides in their capacity for understanding the world, for achieving scientific comprehension of the structure of natural and historical movements, for cooperating consciously with its causes, for making themselves deliberate and intelligent parties to the operation of those causes. Freedom is rational knowledge of the world and hence intelligent action in that world. Without such knowledge, one is history's pawn, pushed this way and that, a manipulated object, an erratic and irrational responder, a highly dependent and unfree person.

According to Marx, if one has social and scientific knowledge of the world, one is capable of acting ethically—that is, striving for what can be achieved. At the same time, however, one knows how little is possible, one knows the severe constraints imposed by history and nature, and one knows one's duty—the "circle of necessity" within which one must act. Thus, in duty one finds one's liberation from dependence on mere impulse. To be free is to know the constraints of necessity.

Even though one is free to choose, if the choices made are often capricious, irrational, based on superstitions and dogma, or unreasonably selfish, then one cannot be called a free person. Inasmuch as Marxists believe that capitalism promotes mystification and alienated behavior, then the masses cannot be free no matter how many voluntary exchanges are permitted or free choices made available.

Thus, although many people in capitalist societies see freedom as "let me alone," Marxists view it as "let me cooperate intelligently with the laws of historical change and eventual liberation." It is this view that leads Marxists to proclaim higher freedoms in communist lands, despite the chains of restraint that encircle the people of those countries. (For Marx's and Engels' views of freedom, see Vernon Venable, Human Nature: The Marxian View, *1966.)*

The Ordeal and Dilemma of Communism

From a starting point of poverty, a young communist country faces an almost impossible task of reaching both much higher living standards and a sustainable socialist society. The active pursuit of either goal endangers the attainment of the other.

A sustainable socialism must have democratic features to elicit the continuing support of the populace. But people in an underdeveloped country can carry out a revolution and attain Marxist socialism only under the leadership of a vanguard communist party. This is a necessity that is opposed to the democracy and freedoms demanded by the working classes in communist countries.

In general, the communist countries have had slower economic growth since the early 1970s, which can be traced partly to weaknesses in their central planning and other socialist policies, and partly to adverse external factors. The internal factors, therefore, are not entirely responsible for the mounting problems of most of the communist countries. When one considers the economic growth performances of the mature communist countries throughout the postwar period, one has to accord them fairly high marks. Although communist living standards are still substantially below those in advanced capitalist societies, the growth rates of these latecomers suggest that this is not the area of their greatest weakness.

The mature communist countries have attained or approached industrial economies and higher living standards at the expense of acceptable and endurable socialist societies. They have industrialized, or are on their way to this result, in a nonsocialist way. Their failure to attain viable socialist societies is their prime deficiency.

The presence of capitalism and the pattern of its development over the centuries have aided in turning the socialism of Marx and Engels into what must be called nonsocialism, and in weakening Marxist regimes as conveyors of socialist economic development. The ordeal of communism lies in the rough road ahead. Communism's future lies in the hands of its working classes who, reaching up for communism's promises, can seek to thoroughly transform their societies, or who, succumbing even more deeply to communism's oppression, can reach up with outstretched arms only for help.

The United States and the Soviet Union exchange signals over the abyss. (Drawing by Eugene Mihaesco.)

7

The Three Worlds:
Problems and Prospects

THE FIRST WORLD OF ADVANCED CAPITALISM, the Second World of communism, and the Third World of noncommunist less-developed countries are all experiencing serious problems at the present time. Because the three worlds have many economic and financial transactions with one another, the problems of each world have close connections with the problems of the others. Furthermore, the prospects of any of these worlds overcoming its problems depend partly on the course of events in the other areas of the globe, as well as on its own circumstances and policies.

In this final chapter we shall review each world's difficulties and examine the remedies available as well as the remedies now being used to eliminate or at least ameliorate the ills. We shall, in closing, assess the prospects facing each of these worlds, especially the communist countries.

The Problems of the First World

The weakness of the First World is the contentious disunity within each of the major capitalist countries, among many of these countries themselves, and between these countries and other nations of the world. The multiplication of economic and political power centers within and without the advanced capitalist countries has led to struggles over shares of national and world incomes. In these struggles, owners of capital have lost ground to their domestic opponents, the U.S. and British capitalists have been weakened by their German and Japanese competitors, and the advanced capitalist countries as a group have yielded some of their power to global Marxism, rising nationalism, and the rich oil-exporting countries. The domestic and international losses have weakened owners of capital, causing lower rates of capital formation and economic growth, and the continuing conflicts over income shares have, at the same time, led to inflation. Thus, stagflation reflects the relative decline of the managers and owners of capital within the context of disunity.

The principal predicament of the First World is that, since economic progress depends on strong, innovative, and enterprising capitalist classes, the fact that these classes have lost some vigor in the past few decades endangers the future of advanced capitalist countries. Capitalism without strong capitalists is an enfeebled system. Capitalism split into numerous contending groups is a society adrift, without consensual aims.

The Prospects of the First World

There are several possible outcomes to the principal predicament of the First World, each of which flows from certain remedial policies:

1. The continuation of the debility of capitalist classes and, consequently, of slow economic growth punctuated by bouts of inflation and waves of unemployment.

2. The strengthening of managers and owners of capital by:
• redistributions of income in their favor, the withdrawal of much government involvement in their affairs, and policies to stimulate work, saving and investment, and risk taking; and
• the weakening of domestic and foreign groups contending against the capitalist classes.

3. The depreciation or displacement of capitalist classes by:
• an augmented government-business partnership in which the capitalist state undertakes and supports much of capital formation on behalf of capital-owning classes;
• social democratic, socialist, or labor governments that represent primarily the working classes, but also capitalists, within an essentially capitalist society; and
• Marxist-socialist or communist governments that represent the working classes, and not the capitalists, within a Marxist society.

Maintaining the Status Quo

Although the managers and owners of capital no longer constitute a robust class that, without opposition, defines society's goals, fashions a consensus around them, and leads the nation to their fulfillment, this class still controls much of economic and political life and continues to dominate the working classes. As a consequence, all of the advanced capitalist societies could continue into the future much as they have proceeded in the recent past—with a hobbled leading class carrying out just enough capital formation to provide a modicum of economic progress over the long run. In shorter periods, sequences of slumps and prosperities would persist, with the downturns becoming more frequent and more pronounced and the upturns becoming less vigorous. Although, in this manner, capitalism could endure for some time to come, a crippled capitalism would probably become more contentious as well as more unstable.

Reinvigorating the Capitalist Classes

A strengthened leading class would enable each of the advanced capitalist societies to regain its more vigorous pace of economic and social development. Rising profits to owners of capital would be the agent of this reinvigoration. Expanding capital formation, faster economic growth, rising employment levels, firmer leadership, and, perhaps, even more social harmony would be the results.

A possible solution, therefore, to the main problems of the First World is the strengthening of the capital-owning classes by government policies that relieve them of onerous state regulations and controls, heavy taxes, rapid inflation and high interest rates, and abnormal risks of investment. The Reagan program in the United States and the Thatcher policies in Great Britain have been designed along these lines, with the chief aims of raising profit expectations of the owners and managers of capital and thus stimulating new capital formation and the growth of output and jobs.

These administrations have also attempted to constrain the main adversaries of the capital-owning classes—labor in particular in Great Britain; labor, consumer-interest groups, environmentalists, and others in the United States. In addition, the Reagan administration has set out to strengthen U.S. capitalism in the world at large by policies to damage unfriendly regimes, such as aid to the opponents of the Sandanistas in Nicaragua and assistance to opponents of communist regimes in Southeast Asia, by the expansion of rapid deployment forces and other military hardware, and by trade measures that diminish "unfair" competition from Japanese, German, and other commercial rivals.

Both the Reagan and Thatcher plans seek to reduce or redesign welfare and income-maintenance programs and rationalize tax structures in ways that will stimulate work and discourage leisure and welfare loafing, increase saving and deter consumption, and boost risk taking by capital owners by checking the use of safe havens and tax shelters for capital and rewarding positively those who gain by taking chances. The Reagan course envisages a robust capitalist class that stands on its own feet without unwarranted aid from the government—that is, private enterprisers reinvigorated as government releases its grip and steps back, after providing the profit seekers with sufficient profit opportunities. President Reagan told an audience of businessmen in November 1982, in connection with a new jobs training act: "This time you, the private employers of America, will lead, not the federal government. Do what you do best. Be leaders."

Conservative critics of social-security systems claim that these programs discourage work and saving, contribute heavily to government budget deficits and, hence, to more inflation and higher interest rates, and, by these and other means, weaken private enterprise. Accordingly, several advanced capitalist societies, with managed economies and generous welfare systems, have recently reduced their managing and become less generous. In the Netherlands, for instance, where employers and employees contributed about 60 percent of total payrolls in 1982 to finance the social-security system, the center-right coalition, which came into power in late 1982, revealed plans to reduce government spending, especially on welfare, to stimulate industrial activity and jobs. The ten capitalist members of the European common market in 1982 allocated 26 percent of their gross national products to their social-security programs (the figure is about 10 percent for the United States), which many of them considered to be excessive in view of rising government deficits and lagging investment and growth rates. In Belgium and Norway, social and welfare programs recently lost favor with the voters and new directions were worked out to stimulate private economic activity.

Although capitalist governments usually act in the interest of owners and managers of capital, conflicts have arisen occasionally between the two sides. For example, the Reagan administration and its predecessors sometimes sought to hamper world communism with embargoes, other trade restrictions, and credit curbs. But these policies also had the short-run effect of injuring some domestic businesses and farmers, and they had the longer-term danger of allowing foreign competitors to capture the markets of U.S. exporters. Similarly, U.S. bankers and industrialists have often favored stability in communist countries where they have business interests over the instability attending uprisings against the communist parties and governments of those countries. Consequently, when the U.S. government has chosen to back such uprisings in the hope of eliminating or greatly modifying the communist regimes, some U.S. enterprisers have found themselves on the other side of the fence. Thus, Solidarity, the independent trade union movement in Poland, was applauded and supported by the Reagan administration, but it was not vigorously defended by many bankers, and actually was opposed by some, after the Polish government was unable to meet payments on its foreign debts.

The managers and owners of capital, therefore, sometimes have different notions from their governments regarding what public actions will or will not strengthen them. This difference of opinion is also found among capitalist governments—as when the Reagan administration set out to punish the Soviet Union for its intervention in Polish affairs by denying it equipment and material from U.S. companies and their foreign subsidiaries and licensees for use on the Siberian gas pipeline project, an action opposed by most of the Western European leaders. In November 1982, within six months of the imposition of these economic sanctions and after much divisiveness over this action both in the United States and abroad, the U.S. sanctions were lifted. They were replaced by a broadly framed agreement among the allies regarding conditions of East-West trade, including the pledge "not to engage in trade arrangements which contribute to the military or strategic advantage of the U.S.S.R. or serve to preferentially aid the heavily militarized Soviet economy."

The Diminution or Displacement of Capitalist Classes

Other possible outcomes of the predicament of the First World include policies to reduce or eliminate the role of owners and managers of capital in the economic life of the nation. The reduced role for entrepreneurial decision making could be achieved by an augmented government role in matters of capital formation, labor relations, and research and development. The vehicle for this outcome would be a strong government-business partnership (perhaps including labor, too) in which the government directly participates in some of the capital formation and supports much of the rest of it undertaken by private enterprise. This support can include protection against competing imports, subsidized interest costs, guarantees against some potential causes of failure, the provision of complementary capital projects, lower taxes, shared equity ownership, and the like. Such a partnership would aim to save the capitalist system through state support of a faltering capitalist class.

Social democratic, socialist, and labor parties have sought to revitalize capitalist economies by more forcefully representing the interests of the working classes without withdrawing all support from the capital-owning classes. These governments have attempted to "get the economy moving again" with expansionary fiscal and monetary policies along Keynesian lines while, at the same time, meeting some of the most pressing demands of labor—for higher wages, shorter work weeks, and improved social-security programs. The results—as in Great Britain with the Labour party, in France with the Mitterand socialist government, and in Scandinavia with various leftist administrations—have usually been to fuel the inflationary furnace without achieving compensatory gains in output and employment, or to discourage even further the engine of progress still located in the private business and financial sectors. This "solution," in effect, has been to spread economic power and leadership of the nation among capitalists, workers, and the government, with the usual result that there is no real leadership at all.

Finally, capitalist classes could conceivably be ousted entirely from political power and replaced by a Marxist-socialist or communist party representing exclusively the working classes. This action would obviously solve the problem of weak capitalist classes. However, in Chapter 3 we saw compelling reasons why revolutionary Marxism is not at all likely to be successful in the advanced capitalist world. Except in Italy and to a smaller degree in France, communism has very little support in Western Europe, North America, Japan, Australia, and New Zealand. These economies would have to be on the verge of collapse—which would be most unlikely—before communism could become a potent political force within them.

The Probable Future

The Reagan and Thatcher programs, in which the government retreats to allow more room for private enterprise, depend for their success on the extent to which capital-owning classes can be revitalized. The analysis in Chapter 5 suggested that this revitalization would be difficult, though not impossible, to achieve. As we saw there, capitalism's weakness lies largely in its disunity, manifested in increasing tensions among contending groups and in bouts of increasing inflation and weakening growth. The correctives required are greater strength to the capitalist classes relative to their opponents, less contention and more agreement among all groups about the leading role of capital, and the reinforcement of world capitalism in its contest with communism. This is a tall order. Whether policies such as those of the Reagan and Thatcher administrations will be able to achieve these correctives is in doubt.

In fact, such government programs, however determinedly focused they are in the beginning, soon become diluted and distorted precisely because of pressures arising from the disunity and contentiousness that they seek to correct. The political scientist Samuel H. Beer has recently argued in *Britain Against Itself* (1982) that in Britain—and he surmises in other advanced capitalist countries as well, especially the United States—there has developed "a paralysis of public choice," an inability of the government to legislate a consistently focused program of any importance. He traces this paralysis to the fragmentation of the decision-making system which has impaired its ability to act in the long-run interests of its members. The fragmentation in turn has grown out of the "decline of the civic culture"— the crumbling of the cement holding society together. The agent of this fragmentation has been a new populism that stresses direct-action protests and the rejection of hierarchies of any kind. Beer's judgment is that these forces make it extremely difficult for society to achieve anything resembling a consensus among the contending groups, even when each group believes that such a consensus would be in its own interest.

The disunity within the capitalist world, therefore, not only accounts, as argued previously, for many of the economic problems of capitalism, but, as Beer would have it, the fragmentation also makes it extremely difficult for an administration to legislate a coherent program to solve the problems.

Gray Panthers in front of the White House take to the street their fears regarding changes in Social Security (November 1982). (Walker—Liaison)

A likely outcome of the predicament of the First World is that the contentious disunity that besets these countries will persist. If the programs to strengthen the capital-owning classes do not succeed, given the difficulties that stand in the way of their implementation, governments will most likely step in to bolster the unsteady owners of capital. These government incursions into the private sectors will probably occur sporadically (as with the U.S. government's involvement with Lockheed, Chrysler, savings and loan associations, steel imports, and so on), until an augmented government-business partnership has been formed, in which the government has become the senior partner. If this prospect is realized, policies such as those of the Reagan and Thatcher administrations will be seen as little more than aberrations from the main course that history has laid out for the First World.

The Problems of the Second World

Revolutionary Marxism was denied a home in the domain of advanced capitalism but found fertile ground instead in the less-developed areas of the world, where the colonial powers, with their imperial and imperious activities, prepared the way for revolution. However, as we observed in Chapter 6, a young communist country, starting from a position of poverty in the underdeveloped world, faces a virtually impossible dual task of reaching much higher standards of living and a sustainable socialist society. The active pursuit of either goal alone endangers the attainment of the other, and the active pursuit of both goals together has proven to be an accomplishment outside the reach of these regimes.

Moreover, as we have also seen, sustainable Marxist-socialist societies demand democratic features to elicit the continuing support of the working classes. These societies came into being, however, in milieus that had their own demands: that communist revolutions would succeed only if powerful vanguard parties led the masses to victory. After the revolutionary triumphs, the vanguard communist parties consolidated and expanded their forces for the next assault—the attainment of economic development and socialism. Thus, the working classes were effectively removed from the levers of political and economic control, and almost all power resided, and continues to reside, in the party-state bureaucracies.

The older communist countries of the Second World have already covered an astonishing amount of ground in their developmental journeys, even though they have only walked in recent years when formerly they ran. But those countries have not been able, at the same time, to fashion endurable socialist societies acceptable to their working classes. Instead, the party-state bureaucracies have achieved much higher levels of production, substantial gains in industrialization, and somewhat higher standards of living, by means that can only be called authoritarian and nonsocialist. Equally disquieting, as we shall see, are the indications that, even if the advanced capitalist countries regain their health and buy and invest more heavily in the Second World, many of the communist countries have encountered so many internal problems that their old economic momentum, within existing structures, probably cannot be regained.

These arguments suggest that the principal predicament of the Second World is that further economic progress and a maintainable and acceptable socialism depend on the vigorous leadership of the working classes. However, these classes have been submerged by the growing deadweight of the bureaucracies. Marxist-socialist societies without strong working classes are crippled systems, vulnerable to economic stagnation, social decay, and disunity both domestic and international.

The Prospects of the Second World

The principal predicament of the Second World can be effectively resolved within the socialist model only if the workers overthrow the party-state bureaucracies and take possession of political power themselves. After that, the workers would have to transform the existing models of economic development into developmental modes that lead not only to further gains in living standards but also to sustainable socialist societies, of the type discussed in Chapter 2.

The Stalinist model of socialist economic development was adopted by the Soviet Union in the late 1920s and early 1930s. It was imposed on most of Eastern Europe after World War II and urged on, and accepted by, the Chinese during the 1950s. Other countries, such as Mongolia, North Korea, and Cuba, have used all or major parts of this model for their own development. However, after Stalin's death in 1953, many of these countries, including the Soviet Union, carried out reforms of the Stalinist model and experimented with alternative practices and institutions—but only within the context of the continued domination of the party-state bureaucracies over the working classes. Some of the reforms were successful and were later improved and then carried over to the present day. Others fell short of their promises or failed to obtain sufficient political support, in which event the countries reverted to some of the basic features of the Stalinist framework.

At the present time, the Stalinist model is found, in modified forms, in some of the older communist countries, including the Soviet Union, East Germany, Albania, Bulgaria, and North Korea. Other countries, such as Yugoslavia, Hungary, Czechoslovakia, and China, are currently employing even more reformed versions of the Stalinist model—so reformed, in fact, that their models of development might well go under their own names. In a more radical departure, many of the Polish workers in 1980–81 challenged the political and social power of the party bureaucracies themselves, demanding a share of that power.

The actual course of recent events, therefore, informs us about the various prospects of the Second World. In examining these prospects, it is best to begin with the Stalinist model. The possible prospects for the Second World include the return to that model, the further reform or even abandonment of it, and working-class revolts against both the Stalinist model (or its reformed versions) and the accompanying monopoly of political and social power held by the party-state bureaucracies.

The Stalinist Model

The Stalinist model of economic development is an all-out, forced march to industrial power through the media of socialist institutions—nationalized industries, collectivized agriculture, and national planning. This model seeks to achieve industrial power by favoring industry over agriculture, heavy industry (producer goods) over light industry (consumer goods), investment over consumption, urban over rural development, quantitative gains over quality improvements, and large capital-intensive projects over small labor-intensive undertakings. The original model strove for military might by basing weapons production on the heavy industrial base and favoring military over civilian output.

The Stalinist model also accepted growing inequalities of wealth and status, the assembling of immense bureaucracies, and the fashioning of a labor aristocracy and a managerial elite. It included sizable numbers of forced laborers, labor camps, and much oppression. The communist party ruled, enterprise managers conformed and passed on the decrees, and the workers were degraded to carrying out the orders. Centralized administrative planning determined almost all of the key economic decisions.

The Return to the Stalinist Model

No communist country today employs the Stalinist model in the manner that Stalin did during the 1930s and 1940s. Even those countries that still conform to several parts of the model, and certainly the other communist countries, give more attention to consumer goods and food supplies than Stalin did, engage more in international trade and foreign borrowing, make more decisions at lower planning levels, rely on market processes to a greater extent, give more autonomy to industrial and trading enterprises, strive for more equality of incomes, and exert less political oppression on their citizens.

The departures from the Stalinist model of the 1930s are now so numerous, and there are currently so many more experiences for new communist regimes to draw on, including those of China, Cuba, Yugoslavia,

144

and Hungary, that no country is likely to return to that austere and regimented path of the Soviets—not even the Soviet Union itself.

It must be remembered, though, that certain features of Stalin's policies of the 1930s continue to influence all communist countries, including Stalin's basic measures leading to nationalization of industry, collectivization of agriculture, and national planning. Stalin's emphasis on military production has also been carried over to the present day.

Further Reforms of the Stalinist Model

The most likely immediate prospect for the Second World is the persistence of reforms of, and experiments with, socialist planning systems—all of them, however, conducted within the political framework that prevents the working classes from exercising true leadership.

National planning through socialist institutions is not an easy task. Socialist planning requires a set of objectives, such as the production of certain amounts of steel, coal, consumer goods, and food for the purpose of achieving a target growth rate of gross national product within a context of stable prices. To produce the target amount of steel, however, requires knowledge of the factor inputs needed for such a task, such as coal and workers of various skills. Sufficient coal must be produced not only for steel but also for the production of food and consumer goods. Coal is also needed to produce coal—and steel is required for that purpose, too. These interdependencies form a grid of input and output relations, industry by industry, that become increasingly difficult to specify as the economy grows more complex.

National planners also know that there are many ways to produce any particular commodity—for example, with much labor and little capital, or the reverse, or combinations in between. The choice depends largely on the price of one factor relative to the price of the other. But these prices, if they are to be helpful guides, must reflect the relative scarcities of the factors. For example, if labor is plentiful and capital goods are not, the price of labor should be low relative to that of capital goods—to induce the planners and others to use labor whenever they can and avoid the use of capital goods. Moreover, the managers of state enterprises must have the proper guidelines and incentives to produce the planned amounts of output in the least expensive way and to turn out products that are wanted by the potential buyers. Workers in the state enterprises and peasants in agricultural cooperatives must also have incentives to work hard and to improve their skills. And, once the goods are produced, they must be distributed to the right places.

In the face of such demanding tasks, many things can go wrong. Plans may be specified incorrectly, too much coal may be produced and too little food, prices may not be established at the right levels to reflect true scarcities, plant managers may be induced to act contrary to the plans, and consumers may be dissatisfied with the low quality of goods in the stores. The Stalinist model is especially difficult to implement because it requires that most of the decisions be made within the planning bureaus, not in the markets, and that most of these decisions be made at the center of the planning structure, not at lower levels. This model also demands that as much output as possible be squeezed from the production system. The Stalinist model calls for such tight central planning that little room is left in it to absorb errors.

In these circumstances, most of the communist countries, having originally adopted the Stalinist model, or something close to it, began almost immediately to reform it. These reforms have been of four types.

Planning reorganizations. The first type of reform has reorganized national planning establishments, often by reshuffling ministries, and has reordered planning priorities. The search has been for greater efficiency in decision making, but the results have often been more cosmetic than substantive, more disappointing than satisfying.

One of the most famous planning reorganizations was carried out by Nikita Khrushchev in the Soviet Union during 1957, when he changed the planning structure from a ministerial (or vertical) to a territorial (or horizontal) system. In the former system, each ministry was in charge of a certain sector of industry, commerce, or agriculture. The State Planning Commission coordinated the activities of the various ministries, each of which had under it all the enterprises producing the goods (such as machine tools) that it supervised. In the latter system, regional councils replaced the ministries, and each council coordinated all industries, of whatever type, and other economic activities in its territorial unit. In 1965, a year after the fall of Khrushchev, the system was returned to the ministerial form.

Decentralization of decision making and management. The second type of reform has involved decentralization of decision making and management within the given planning structure. Since, in the Stalinist model, the key decisions are made at the top and handed down, these reforms have transferred some of the decisions to lower levels of planning. Often, too, the management of state enterprises, originally performed by state authorities, has been turned over to local jurisdictions. All communist countries have engaged in these and similar reforms. In each case, the aim has been to improve the quality of decisions and managerial services by locating them closer to the scenes of action. Not infrequently, however, disappointing results and mounting planning disharmonies have caused the return of some or all of these activities back to the central authorities. These reversions occurred in Poland, East Germany, and Hungary during the late 1950s and in the Soviet Union during the 1960s.

Decontrol. The third type of reform has been that of decontrol. These reforms have moved many decisions out of national planning structures entirely and have permitted them to be made by enterprises, families, and individuals. The reforms have encouraged enterprises to buy and sell more freely—to buy the raw materials and labor that they need, and to sell the goods that they produce either to domestic or to foreign markets—and to retain more of their profits, which they can then distribute as bonuses to workers, set aside in welfare and other funds, or invest in new capital equipment and structures. These reforms have also relieved planners of setting prices on certain consumer goods, leaving it to individual buyers and sellers of these goods to establish prices for them through market processes. The assignment of workers to jobs has sometimes been removed from officials and handed over to the workers themselves, who have become free to seek their own positions. Each of these changes reduces the scope of central planning and raises the role of market processes—that is, of microplanning by firms and families. When a communist country carries out extensive reforms of this type, it is said to move from a command economy to market socialism.

An outstanding instance of this sort of transformation was afforded by the Hungarian economic reforms of 1968, which were accomplished by the Communist party under the leadership of János Kádár, and which that country termed the New Economic Mechanism (NEM). The NEM dismantled much of the central-planning structure and turned many of the erstwhile planning decisions on investment, production, and prices over to the individual enterprises. The enterprises were more or less pushed out into the competitive world to live or die in the race for profits. However, the new system produced growing disparities of income, profiteering, and some unemployment. In response to these problems, the government in 1973 increased its control over investment and prices and resumed its protection of some of the weaker firms. Since 1973 there have been further reforms, the principal aim of which has been to raise the efficiency of the economy and hence its rate of growth. But reforms of decontrol have threatened workers with unemployment, some managers with failure, and many planners with loss of power. Such reforms have also favored the industrious, the skilled, and the lucky, and so they have worsened the distribution of income. By relying more on market operations, the reforms have led to open inflation of prices. Consequently, strong opposition groups have been formed against the decontrol measures, not only in Hungary but in several other communist countries as well.

Another dramatic example of reforms of decontrol was Yugoslavia's move, beginning in 1950 under Marshall Tito (Josip Broz), to workers' self-management of enterprises. This arrangement gave workers, through their work councils and directors, the power to make decisions regarding the operations of their enterprises, including the pricing and marketing of the articles produced, the investment or other disposition of aftertax profits and other funds, the setting of wage rates, and the choice of technology to be used in production. In 1965 Yugoslavia extended decontrol mainly by transferring much of the supervision of investment funds from the central government budget to the banking system, and by elevating the role of markets in other ways.

Nevertheless, because the banks are subject to central influence and control, the Yugoslavian government has retained much power over aggregate investment in the economy. The government has apparently also exerted its influence on the directors of enterprises. Despite the enhanced position of the working classes in Yugoslavia, they do not control the main levers of politics and economics. The League of Communists (the Communist party) and the government are still in political control of the state, and these bodies continue to dominate the momentous economic decisions.

Desocialization of the economy. The fourth type of reform—the most radical of the group—has endorsed desocialization of the economy. These reforms have encouraged small private enterprises in retail trade, repairs, food production, restaurants, and manufacturing. They have also opened the door to foreign private investment. In addition, the reforms have transformed higher levels of socialization to lower ones, such as state farms to cooperatives, state enterprises to locally owned firms, and the income-distribution units from larger to smaller socialist groups. The purposes of such measures have been to advance economic activity in areas not covered by socialist institutions, to stimulate individual incentives in the hope of attaining higher growth rates, and to engage the services of foreign experts and tap foreign technology.

Poland and Yugoslavia, for example, in the 1950s reversed their drives to collectivize agriculture by turning back to private farming. Since Mao's death, especially since 1978, China has sanctioned small private businesses, mainly in the services sectors. In the last few years, China has also encouraged private investment from abroad, reduced the effective sizes of socialist units in the countryside, and furthered private sideline activities among the peasants, such as raising pigs, growing fruit and vegetables, and making household utensils and other handicraft items. Similar reforms were carried out in the early 1920s by Lenin in the young Soviet Union, in the early 1980s by the socialist government in the West African country of Guinea, and by many communist parties in between.

As we noted earlier, almost all of the communist countries are currently beleaguered by slow rates of growth, growing inefficiencies, and other stresses and strains. As a consequence, most of them will persevere in seeking reforms of their socialist-planning systems. They will not return to the Stalinist model. But some of the countries, notably the Soviet Union, may continue to revamp their planning agencies by juggling ministries and interchanging the various pieces of these structures. Other countries, such as Albania, may be compelled to decentralize decision making more than they already have within a given planning system, while Poland and Cuba may seek their salvations more than ever outside of the planning system, in the competitive world of markets and prices. The more desperate countries may partially reverse the degree of socialization in their economies by encouraging private enterprise in limited areas, as China has been doing.

The last two types of reform—decontrol and desocialization—are definitely retreats, temporary and strategic as they may be, from the socialist model that is identified with Marx and Engels—the model set forth in Chapter 2. These reforms are retreats because they diminish the role of national planning and sacrifice some social ownership of the means of production, two of the core elements of a socialist society. The purpose of these reforms is to boost the efficiency of the economy and so raise production and standards of living, and such reforms have frequently attained these goals. The dangers of such policies to the existing communist regimes is that they strengthen politically an increasingly prosperous and economically powerful group of capital owners, private entrepreneurs, technocrats, managers, speculators, and financiers, and by so doing increase the chances for the restoration of some type of capitalist system.

Nevertheless, communist countries will continue their search for a strategy that will achieve both higher living standards and an endurable socialism. That strategy has yet to be discovered.

Workers' Revolts

The accumulating economic and social problems of the communist countries have been met by the ruling regimes partly with the reforms just discussed. These problems have concerned not only the bureaucrats, but also have had serious adverse effects on the working classes of these countries. The economic difficulties have prevented increases in workers' living standards—and at times have even reduced them. The social environment has been oppressive in that the ruling regimes have denied the workers the rights to organize in opposition to, and independently of, the government and to strike, to speak freely, to hear and read all the news without censorship or lies, and to have a voice in the decisions affecting conditions of their work and retirement.

Thus, the workers have sometimes taken matters into their own hands by revolting against the deteriorating conditions and even, upon occasion, against "the system." Workers' revolts occurred in Czechoslovakia and East Germany in 1953, Poland and Hungary in 1956, Czechoslovakia again in 1968 (when an alliance was struck between students and trade unionists in the wake of the removal of Alexander Dubček), Poland in 1970 and again in 1976, Rumania in 1977–79, and finally in Poland once more in August 1980, at which time the independent trade union, Solidarity, was born. There have also been reports of revolts and strikes by workers in both the Soviet Union and China. However, Poland has had more than its share of such uprisings (even when we exclude the student demonstrations of 1968, which failed to elicit the support of the workers).

Poland in the 1950s. The Stalinist epoch in Poland lasted from 1949 to the mid-1950s. During 1955–56 the Polish United Workers' party (the Communist party) tentatively reduced some of the Stalin-like oppression that it had imposed on the society. In February 1956 Khrushchev denounced the crimes of Stalin. These events led to the rebellion of workers—against low real wages, excessive production targets, and the Russian yoke—in a few urban areas and to the subsequent establishment of workers' councils (inspired by Yugoslavia's enterprises under workers' management) in many more locales. But these uprisings were more directed by the intelligentsia than by the workers themselves, who had at that time little organization or leadership from their own ranks.

Poland in the 1960s. During the 1960s, the Polish economy grew by about 6 percent per year, which was quite high by world standards. However, Poland's industrial sector accounted for most of the overall gains, for agricultural output barely grew at all over the decade, actually declining in the last few years of the 1960s. Moreover, industry utilized large amounts of capital goods relative to labor, which required, as the 1960s went on, increasing imports to sustain the growth—for Poland was not capable of producing all these capital goods itself. Poland's international balance of trade, therefore, went into deficit, reflecting more imports than exports. The planning system was also under increasing pressure throughout the decade, as it was not able to keep abreast of the structural changes in the economy that accompanied the growth.

At the end of the 1960s, the Communist party initiated a series of economic reforms of decentralization and decontrol. The party also began to increase and concentrate investment expenditures with the intention of modernizing critical areas of the economy. The investment funds were diverted from housing, consumption goods, and other social programs into electronics, machine tools, and chemicals. The rising incomes in the economy generally, poor harvests, and food prices that were set too low by the government (to placate the workers) resulted in excess demands for (and hence shortages of) meat and other food products.

The abnormally low administered prices for meat and other foods in Poland—and in other Eastern European countries, too—reflected the fear by the government of workers' responses to higher prices. These low prices set by the government were a manifestation of disunity within the social fabric of society. Just as social disunity in capitalist countries, when market prices are free to rise, is evidenced in open inflation, social disunity in communist countries, under conditions of controlled prices, is manifested in long queues at butcher shops and grocery stores, in shortages, unrest, and suppressed inflation.

The anxiety of Polish bureaucrats regarding the consequences of increases in meat prices flowed from fervent demands by the workers. The journalist Neal Ascherson, in *The Polish August* (1982), stated that: "There was something irrational, even aggressive, about the carnivorous obsession that now gripped the Poles. Their per capita meat consumption was higher than that of several [much richer] Western countries, and their insistence on pork at the expense of more plentiful meats like beef or lamb led to queues and shortages. In an act of subconscious aggression, the population was literally eating away the foundations of the political structure." Such behavior is itself a response to the frustrations of social discord.

On Saturday, December 12, 1970, the government unexpectedly announced price increases on certain foods, along with price adjustments, up and down, on other consumer goods. On the following Monday, workers began protesting these measures, and strikes and demonstrations broke out in Gdansk, Gdynia, and Szczecin, port cities on the Baltic Sea. The rebellion spread to other cities and in a short time work was halted, in a spontaneous series of stoppages, throughout the country. In the wake of these protests, Wladyslaw Gomulka, leader of the Communist party, was forced out, and he was replaced by Edward Gierek, who appealed directly to the workers for their understanding and patriotism, and who met some of the workers' grievances by abrogating the price increases. Before long, the workers went back to work.

Ascherson, in the work cited above, stated that the meaning of the 1970 events was that for the first time "a Communist government had been overthrown directly by the action of the industrial proletariat." Ascherson also noted that "among the twenty-one demands drawn up by the Szczecin strikers there figured for the first time the call for 'independent trade unions under the authority of the working class.' " After 1970, Ascherson concluded, the working class understood that it "could frustrate any measure by taking to the streets with sufficient energy."

Poland in the 1970s. During the next four or five years, the Polish economy surged ahead on the basis of Gierek's new policies to modernize the industrial sector by importing modern technology and plant from the West, financed by substantial foreign borrowing. The debts were to be paid by rising exports of coal, copper, sulphur, ships, and the products of the modernized industrial sector. From 1971 through 1975, Poland's national output rose by about 10 percent a year, which was close to the highest growth rate in the world at that time. The average real wage of workers

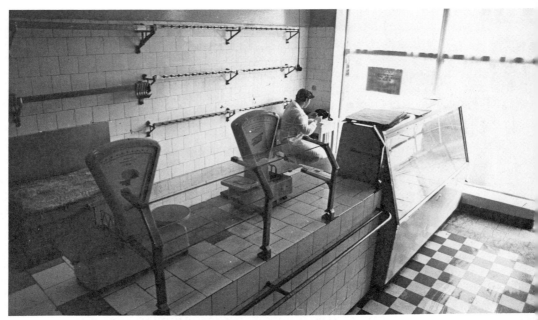

Top: An empty butcher shop in suburban Warsaw. (Laffont—Sygma) Bottom: A Solidarity rally in Warsaw, 1981. (Philippot—Sygma)

also jumped sharply—between 35 and 40 percent in those five years. The government supported a new housing program and increased welfare and health benefits for the workers, whose living standards markedly improved. By 1975, Poland was producing the twelfth largest gross national product in the world—just behind Spain and Brazil, but ahead of Australia, Holland, Sweden, and Mexico. During that brief period in the early seventies, the Poles had the model economy of the entire communist world.

During the second half of the 1970s, however, the economy began to weaken until it stopped growing altogether and then finally all but collapsed. This dramatic turn of fortune was caused by several unfavorable factors that converged in a short span of time: consecutive years of very bad weather for agricultural crops; sharp increases in oil and gas prices; declining rates of growth in the advanced capitalist countries; unrealistic and inconsistent macroplanning by the bureaucracy, including a shift in farm policy from private to socialist agriculture; and demands by workers for wage increases far exceeding productivity gains.

On June 24, 1976, the government raised prices on food and basic consumer goods by substantial amounts—for example, the price of sugar doubled, meat prices rose on the average by about 70 percent, and food prices as a whole jumped 40 percent. Serious disturbances by workers erupted immediately; by the next day work stopped all over the country. The government quickly annulled the price increases but, at the same time, arrested many strikers. Although workers soon went back to their jobs, they began to organize unofficial opposition groups, including the Committee for the Defense of Workers' Rights (KOR) and a Students' Solidarity Committee. In 1977–78 free trade union groups arose, and an informal alliance was struck between these opposition groups and the Catholic Church.

As the economy worsened and food shortages became more frequent, work stoppages erupted once again. Workers complained of widespread corruption and abuses of power within the Communist party, increasing inequalities of income and wealth, shortages of meat (owing, the workers wondered, to shipments to the Moscow Olympics?), and a mounting number of repressive measures and actions by the government. The government's announcement on July 1980 of price increases on meat and meat products (accomplished by transferring certain meats from controlled to commercial markets) triggered another wave of strikes across the country, with each wave of strikers demanding more additional wages than the previous one. As the stoppages spread, the workers' demands broadened: no work on Saturdays, free trade unions, elimination of censorship, and higher family allowances. The opposition group, KOR, became the contact organization that linked the factories together.

The rise of Solidarity. On the morning of August 14, 1980, sixteen thousand workers at the Lenin Shipyard in Gdansk refused to start work and took over the yard. Their initial demands included a large wage increase, the right to form an independent union, and the reinstatement of three recently fired employees. The next day, other workers in Gdansk and Gdynia joined the strike, and a few days later the insurrection reached the Szczecin workers. The Inter-Factory Strike Committee (MKS) was established in Gdansk to coordinate the rapidly spreading strikes and to represent the strikers. By August 22, MKS served four hundred factories and published the first issue of its daily bulletin, which it titled *Solidarity.*

During the first few days of the work stoppages, a thirty-seven-year-old former employee of the Gdansk shipyards but then an unemployed electrician became the leader of the strike at the Lenin facilities. Lech Walesa was born in a farming community about halfway between Warsaw and Gdansk, went to a technical school, and served in the Polish army, in which he earned the rank of corporal. He then became an electrical technician in the shipyards. He was an activist in the December 1970 strikes and was elected by his fellow workers to the strike committee, on which he represented the strikers at a meeting with Edward Gierek in January 1971. During the next worker demonstrations in 1976, Walesa was fired from his job, and for the next four years he found short-term employment wherever he could. He was frequently arrested during this period, but he continued to be active, developing close relations with the opposition group, KOR, and participating in the formation of the Baltic Free Trade Union, which became the nucleus for the Solidarity movement. By backing his friends, Walesa had suffered the consequences, and he was much respected for that.

The Inter-Factory Strike Committee, on behalf of the strikers, presented twenty-one demands to government representatives on August 23, 1980, in Gdansk. In addition to the ones already noted, the demands included the workers' right to participate in open discussions about the declining state of the economy and the programs to correct it, an improvement in health services to assure full medical care to the workers, automatic pay raises indexed to price inflation, a halt to repression against those who oppose government policies, and a rise in the status of women, pensioners, and low-income workers. However, the principal focus of the demands was on the independent trade union, with its right to strike, and increases in living standards, brought about in equitable ways.

An agreement was signed in Gdansk between the workers and the government on August 31. In this document, the government agreed to new self-governing trade unions that would genuinely represent the working class, and to the unions' right to strike. The workers declared, on their part, that the trade unions would not be a political party, and they recognized the leading role of the Communist party. The two sides agreed that the trade unions should have genuine opportunities to participate in the evaluation and formulation of economic policies, including the question of workers' self-government. The government assented to the introduction of a draft law in three months that would ease censorship and political repression. The workers were assured of gradual increases in the wages of all groups of employees, especially among the lowest wage earners, and that the lowest pensions would be raised to some socially acceptable minimum. The government promised to work out by the end of the year the principles of indexing wages to the cost of living and to increase meat supplies; it pledged to improve health services, to introduce as many work-free Saturdays as possible, to increase housing space, and to improve working conditions.

Wildcat strikes continued to break out in the next few weeks, but by September 22 all workers were back on their jobs. On that day, the delegates of thirty-six regional independent unions met at Gdansk and called themselves Solidarity. By late October 1980, membership in Solidarity reached 8 million, and it later rose to 10 million.

During the ensuing months, as the economy plummeted downhill at an ever faster pace, it became increasingly clear that the government was simply unable to make good on all of its promises. The government had agreed in principle to grant the workers fewer days of work, more pay, earlier retirement, higher pensions, and better health care—all of which meant that, although the workers would produce fewer goods and services, they would consume more of the smaller supply. This impasse generated many tensions between the two sides, and strike threats, arrests, and harassments were its manifestations.

During 1981, Solidarity defied the government on many occasions; the government retreated at times and struck back with force, propaganda, and decrees at other times. Solidarity (now including Rural Solidarity, organized by the Polish farmers) held its first national congress in Gdansk in September, in which it put forth a plan for workers' self-management of enterprises and called for more open and authentic voting procedures in the parliamentary elections of 1982. During the summer, the government had produced its own version of a new law on workers' self-management. The parliament, looking at the drafts of both sides, passed a compromise bill on self-management, which was accepted by Solidarity but only with serious reservations.

In the final months of 1981, Solidarity staged several nationwide strikes, and many other work stoppages also occurred, over firings of activists, increases of food prices, low wages and poor working conditions, police repression, and other issues. After months of meetings, Solidarity and the government reached a stalemate in their negotiations for a "national accord," which prompted Walesa to announce on December 10: "We do not want confrontation but we cannot retreat anymore. We cannot be passive any longer as this would be detrimental to the union." A few days before, Walesa had advocated the overthrow of the government, though he charged that the statement was being used out of its context.

The fall of Solidarity. On Saturday night, December 12, 1981, General Wojciech Jarulzelski (who had been appointed first secretary of the Communist party the previous October) declared martial law and the next morning launched a military coup that, over the next few days, resulted in the arrest of almost the entire leadership of Solidarity, including Walesa, and thousands of its members and supporters, who were sent to prison and detention camps. All civil liberties were suspended and all telephone and telegraph communication was halted. Jarulzelski declared a "state of war" and put the government under the direction of a twenty-one-member Army Council of National Salvation. He also arrested Edward Gierek and his senior political colleagues. He asked the workers of Solidarity to have faith in him, for this action, he explained, was intended only to purge the union of a small group of extremists. When this phase was completed, Jarulzelski promised, and order and discipline had been restored, the government would return to economic reforms and further progress, and not to the days before Solidarity.

In October 1982 the Polish parliament outlawed Solidarity. In response, the underground leaders of the union called for a nationwide strike on November 10, but with government force prominently displayed, few workers heeded the call. A few days later, Walesa was released from his eleven-month detention.

Class Relations and Economic Progress

If workers are sufficiently oppressed, they cannot or will not work hard and effectively, and economic progress cannot be achieved. In this case, the workers must overthrow their oppressors to open the way for an era of rapid socialist development. The workers most likely to be able to carry out such a revolution are the industrial proletariat—the urban working class, as exemplified by the shipyard workers of Gdansk. However, the industrial proletariat are the product of economic development itself—of the industrial progress of the economy. Consequently, a working class that is largely without industrial experience and that is greatly oppressed may not be able or willing to carry out the development necessary to transform itself into a revolutionary class. Oppressed workers may simply remain oppressed workers—who have failed not only to attain satisfactory living standards but an acceptable socialist society as well.

This vicious circle is a real danger facing the working classes in some of the more oppressive communist regimes. But it is a circle that can and has been broken. As oppressive as some party-state bureaucracies are, it is nevertheless true that the workers have labored hard enough in many of

156

Lech Walesa talks with a Catholic priest during the strike in the Gdansk shipyard in August 1980. (Poland Watch Center)

these countries to achieve substantial economic gains. This has been true, for example, in Albania, North Korea, and East Germany. The urban working classes have in fact become more numerous in much of the Second World. Indeed, Solidarity in Poland grew as much out of that country's successful economic development as it did out of its political failures. Polish economic development has created an expanding industrial sector and a proletariat to match it. These urban workers have been brought together in large industrial assemblies and so have become aware of themselves as a class and of the Communist party's oppressive weight on them. Solidarity arose from the bowels of heavy industry—in the shipyards, the steel mills, and the other centers of industrial activity.

If industrial progress continues for another few decades in Eastern Europe, the urban working classes will become not only numerically large but also mature in their understanding of their social needs. They will then be a potentially revolutionary force, a greater threat than they now are to the existing communist parties. In years to come, this situation may also arise in China and in other developing communist countries. Numerous and mature urban industrial workers are necessary for the task of overturning the communist bureaucracies, but they do not appear to be sufficient. The Soviet proletariat has yet to arise, and Solidarity's strength was dissipated in its leaders' and members' obedience to the powerful messages from the Catholic Church and the Polish state—messages that apparently touched the very fiber of the Polish soul. They spoke of the unity of all children under God, of the ability of Poles always to be able to reason with Poles, and of workers acting with the national welfare foremost in mind. These messages implicitly warned of the dangers to the nation of class divisions. Solidarity was solid before the cross and the flag, but it was not as solid in fully understanding itself as the social class to lead Poland toward a democratic and prosperous socialist society. However, Solidarity's hesitation before class warfare was also the product of its fear of a Soviet invasion if the trade unionists went too far. The possibility of this dire outcome of precipitous action was used by both church and government to constrain Solidarity.

In the end, the communist bureaucracies can survive only if the economies they administer grow. Protracted economic stagnation could easily bring in the nation's own military or some constellation of antisocialist class forces, such as an alliance of bureaucrats, enterprise managers, and other elites. However, if growth cannot be achieved by measures involving bureaucratic revamping and decentralization of planning—and experience strongly suggests that it cannot—then economic progress will have to be sought with reforms of decontrol and desocialization. If these measures are successful in moving the economy forward, then the party-state bureaucracies will be challenged sooner or later by an expanding class that prospers from its market activities and private-enterprise undertakings. Moreover, as we have just observed, the economic growth will also produce an increasingly strong urban working class that will be capable of issuing challenges of its own. For the present regimes, therefore, there are dangers fore and aft. As the Chinese would say, there is a wolf in the front and a tiger in the rear.

The Problems of the Third World

The main problem of many noncommunist Third World countries is that their "normal" progress has been distorted by the power of larger (or more advanced) nations, power that was exerted in the colonial past and can still be found in the neocolonial present. Many of these Third World countries have been left with no dynamic, dominant social class to take the political reins in the drive for higher living standards. The political vacuums have been filled by weak and shifting coalitions of classes, by foreign capitalists or alien regimes, or by the domestic military forces. In general, these "abnormal" political arrangements have retarded the economic progress of many of the noncommunist less-developed countries.

Military regimes, usually authoritarian and often harsh, have stepped into many of the empty political spaces to represent class or national interests in carrying out economic development programs, such as in Brazil, Indonesia, Libya, Panama, South Korea, Chile, Guatemala, Zaire, and other countries. Some of the military regimes have, for a time, relinquished their overt political power and have allowed nonmilitary coalitions to take over. When they have failed, the military officers have returned. These alternating military and civilian governments have been prominent in Argentina, Turkey, Bolivia, Peru, Niger, Nigeria, Mali, Morocco, and elsewhere. In other cases, such as the Philippines, India, Pakistan, and Ghana, civilian governments have declared martial law for varying periods in order to contain the volatile disequilibrium of class forces. Elsewhere, former colonial nations and present-day capitalist powers continue to exert unusual economic authority over some local economies, making it difficult for them to achieve the indigenous development that would strengthen their capabilities for self-generating growth. Examples of the subordinates of these relations include Puerto Rico, Northern Ireland, the Dominican Republic, Chad, and Zaire. The Soviet Union has also put client states in similar positions—parts of Eastern Europe, Afghanistan, Cuba, and Kampuchea.

These political structures, because of their frailty, brevity of life, and oppressiveness, have contributed to the relatively slow economic growth of the Third World countries taken as a whole. According to the World Bank, from 1960 to 1980 the per capita gross national products of these countries expanded at the average annual rate of only 2.5 to 3 percent. This range compares to over 3.5 percent for the First World and about 4.5

percent for the Second World. If the OPEC countries are separated from the Third World, or if only the very low-income countries of the Third World are considered, the economic comparisons are even more unfavorable to the less-developed countries. On the other hand, some of the most populous Third World countries—Indonesia, Thailand, Nigeria, and Brazil—have unusually high economic growth rates. On the whole, however, the economic performance of the Third World has not only been mediocre but is deteriorating as well.

There are, of course, factors other than the political that account for the relatively poor performances of the Third World group as a whole, including a scarcity of natural resources, poor economic management, high rates of population growth, an inability or unwillingness of their populations to save more, and, in recent years, the sluggish economic progress of the First and Second worlds.

Just as the predicament of the First World lies in the weakening of its leading social class (the owners and managers of capital), and the predicament of the Second World lies in the oppression of the class that should be leading society to its goals (the working class), in the same way the Third World's main predicament lies in the inability in many of these countries of *any* social class to attain dynamic leadership over the others. A weak political superstructure has contributed importantly to a weak economic base.

The Prospects of the Third World

The heterogeneity of the Third World is so pronounced that it is quite risky to assess the prospects of these countries as an entire group. If the countries are ranked by GNP per capita, the bottom third had annual growth rates from 1960 to 1980 of less than 1 percent, the middle third grew by 2.3 percent, and the top third by 4 percent. (These figures are not weighted by the population sizes of the countries.) Thus, on the average, the better off the country, the faster its economy has been growing. Not only are the countries of the First and Second worlds pulling away from those in the Third World, but the Third World itself is like an expanding universe. The economies of Singapore, Hong Kong, Taiwan, South Korea, and several OPEC nations are traveling at great speed at the far reaches of the Third World, while the economies of Chad, Bangladesh, Upper Volta, Haiti, Uganda, Burma, and India (all in the bottom third) are creeping along at a short distance from their starting points. In between these locations with intermediate speeds of growth are Egypt, the Philippines, Morocco, the Ivory Coast, Honduras, and Bolivia (all in the middle third). What can we make of this conglomeration?

First, exceptionally strong forces would be required to alter this configuration in any significant way over the next several decades. Taken as a whole, the Third World probably has little or no chance to catch up to the first two worlds—and, indeed, the most likely prospect is that it will fall farther and farther behind. Also, the Third World itself most likely will continue to fly apart, as just described, with several countries in the top third speeding into the outer expanses now occupied by countries of the First World, but with many more less-fortunate countries trailing far in the rear. The poorest of the poor would seem destined to sink, relatively speaking, into the abyss of economic misery.

Second, inasmuch as part of the predicament of many countries in the Third World lies in their weak political superstructures, the strengthening of them would at least be a step forward. If the impediments of the First World can be overcome by the strengthening of capital-owning classes, if the problems of the Second World can be solved by the strengthening of working classes, then the plight of many Third World countries can be ameliorated if they can replace their ineffective political superstructures with more purposeful and efficient ones. Because these countries have so many problems, this political transformation would probably not be sufficient for overall success, but it might well be necessary.

Third, the countries of the Third World can replace their inefficient political structures only by clearing away the conditions producing them and so opening the way for political parties that know their aims and the means of achieving them and can rally most of the people around such goals. The most likely candidates for these posts are Marxist-Leninist parties, vanguards comprising highly disciplined and dedicated professionals who have an understanding of the class structures of their societies, the peasants' and workers' problems that emanate from these structures, some of the ways of overcoming these problems, and a decidedly socialist orientation.

Under certain circumstances, there are undoubtedly other ways for the people of Third World countries to strengthen their political organs—with a determined military regime, a dictator who rises above class interests and represents the nation as a whole, or a populist party that represents multiple economic interests. However, under many conditions, Marxist-Leninist parties are better equipped—especially when they are supported by the Soviet Union or China—to assume the tasks of revolution.

Fourth, we have already observed that it is virtually impossible for countries, starting from impoverished positions, to attain both higher living standards and a sustainable socialism. Although Marxist-Leninist parties are potent revolutionary weapons, they have had little or no success in achieving rapid socialist development after the revolutions have occurred in poor countries of the Third World.

Finally, we can draw important inferences, framed in the form of questions, from what has just been said: How long will poor people continue to struggle and bleed through Marxist-Leninist revolutions if Marxist parties, after their revolutionary victories, are incapable of achieving substantial increases in living standards for their supporters? And for how long will poor people continue to join revolutions that have ended elsewhere oppressing both peasants and workers beneath all-powerful party bureaucracies? The answers to those questions probably lie in whether there are other escapes for peasants and workers from hunger and oppression and whether there persists a lingering hope—despite the mounting evidence to the contrary—that the future will prove that Marxist-Leninist movements can turn poverty into sufficiency, oppression into liberation.

Speculations

In these final paragraphs, we shall examine some broad and potentially dramatic issues involving the communist countries, issues that are yet to be resolved. This examination is intended to suggest what might happen, based on some—but certainly insufficient—evidence, and the speculations that emerge are themselves challengeable.

The New Europe

The communist countries of Eastern Europe, as we have seen, will probably produce industrial working classes capable of transforming those societies into more democratic forms of socialism. If these workers' revolutions do occur, without a similar revolt in the Soviet Union, the Eastern European countries will find themselves ideologically closer to many of the countries of Western Europe than to the Soviet Union. Short of a thermonuclear war, the Soviet Union may be unable to prevent Eastern Europe from forging ever-closer ties—commercial, cultural, diplomatic, and, eventually, military—with the Western European countries.

At the same time, many of the Western European peoples desire economic societies that are more strongly socialist oriented and that more sympathetically meet the needs of the working classes than the United States would countenance. Moreover, many people in the Western European nations find the political and military weight of the United States in Europe to be unpalatable, an anachronism. There have been increasing disagreements between the United States and some of the Western European governments over policies toward the Soviet Union, on arms control, and on the deployment of nuclear weapons on European soil. More and more, the Western Europeans are going their own way.

There are forces, therefore, repelling both Eastern and Western Europe from their respective control centers. These repellents could be joined by the forces of attraction that arise from the growing similarities between the economies of the two halves of Europe. Both sets of forces together might coalesce to create a new Europe—or, as some scholars describe it, the "Europeanization of Europe."

A New Danger to Democracy

A new danger to democratic institutions in Western Europe is now emerging and may become even more acute. In the future, if Eastern Europe establishes democratic-socialist societies, the danger may spread to those countries, too. If the populations of European nations become rather evenly split between those favoring various types of welfare capitalism and those favoring various types of socialism—as is now true in Britain, France, Scandinavia, Italy, Spain, and elsewhere—there is likely to emerge in each of these countries a damaging and dangerous fragmentation born of divisive swings of the political pendulum: first, let us say, a socialist government, then a capitalist one, then back to another socialist regime, and so on. This alternation of political parties would lead initially to socialist policies of nationalization, economic planning, and improvement in living and working standards for the working classes. These policies could then be followed by capitalist policies of undoing the socialist measures and establishing conditions for freer enterprise and more opportunities for profit making. After that, the socialists could regain political power, and so on.

This political pendulum would be highly disruptive to the economy of any country and so might prevent the countries subject to such oscillation from making any kind of satisfactory economic progress. The political pendulum, it appears, has already harmed the performance of Britain's and Sweden's economies, and if, in a few years from now, a more conservative French administration replaces the socialist Mitterand government, France will experience similar economic and social disruptions. The same may be true, in the years to come, in Spain, Italy, and West Germany.

Although a wide variety of political changes can be implemented to ameliorate this problem, one cure that would undoubtedly ultimately be proposed is the elimination of the democratic institutions giving rise to the problem in the first place. Although it is most unlikely that Western European peoples would accept this solution, it is possible that, if satisfactory economic progress cannot be made, demands will develop and be heeded for some paring of democratic practices and institutions.

The Communist Giants Rejoined

At the close of 1982 there were indications that the Soviet Union and China might develop closer relations once again. The two communist countries split apart in the late 1950s and early 1960s over differences regarding China's economic development policies, leadership claims over the communist world, the more accommodating Soviet policies toward the United States, the Soviets' role in providing China with atomic weapons capability, and other issues. During the 1960s, each side engaged in bitter

The Chinese delegation attending the funeral of the late Soviet President Leonid Breshnev in November 1982. (UPI)

and rancorous denunciations of the other, and in 1969 northern border clashes occurred between their armies. The animosities carried over into the 1970s.

The death of Mao Zedong in 1976 opened the way for policy shifts in this area. Mao's domestic programs and foreign policies were often sharply at odds with the Soviets'. His deep and long-standing distrust of the Russians, his fervent nationalism, and his desire (which began to be expressed after Stalin's death in 1953) that the People's Republic of China should become the new leader of the communist world—all contributed to the growth of ill will between the two nations. Although other Chinese leaders may well continue to hold these same views, Mao's will and influence in these matters were so great that his death allowed the issue of Soviet-Chinese relations to be reopened at last for discussion.

In a world of continuing communist revolutions, there are obvious advantages to both China and the Soviet Union in establishing closer relations, for the two communist countries together could more easily further the spread of Marxism-Leninism around the world than they could separately, as enemies. China also has an interest in displaying her displeasure with U.S. policies toward Taiwan and in putting pressure on the United States to change those policies. The Soviet Union, with its economy under increasing strain, also has an interest in attaining better relations with

China in order to use the resources now being poured into the anti-Chinese military machine for domestic consumption and capital formation. Moreover, the economic basis of the hostility between the two countries has been weakened since Mao's death. The new leaders of China have promoted economic policies that are much more similar to those of the Soviets than were Mao's more leftist policies. Although China still insists that the Soviet Union is "hegemonistic," as evidenced by its policies in Afghanistan, Kampuchea, and on the Soviet-Chinese borders and that these policies must change, the Chinese and the Soviets have compelling reasons for seeking to rejoin hands. Whether the handclasp will be as firm as it was in the 1950s remains to be seen.

Continuing Marxist Revolutions in the Third World

Marxist-Leninist revolutions in the Third World have arisen from the chaos created by wars among capitalist powers, the persistence of colonial empires past their time, economic domination by neocolonial capitalist nations, continuing oppression of people by tyrannical regimes and harsh ruling classes, and the impasse reached by some of these countries in their developmental efforts.

Although the first two factors may no longer apply over the next several decades, the last three factors may persist to be of continuing importance. Furthermore, if the communist parties of the Soviet Union and China establish more normal relations, they could comprise a powerful force in fomenting and supporting revolutions in the Third World. An alliance between the two major communist parties would produce alliances within Third World countries of revolutionary factions that hitherto had reflected the Sino-Soviet split. These local alliances in themselves, even without any further aid or comfort from the Soviets and Chinese, would greatly raise the striking force of Marxism-Leninism and boost morale among the revolutionists of the poor countries. Under these conditions, greater areas of the Third World would become more vulnerable to Marxist-Leninist revolutions.

The Capitalist Americas

Marxist-Leninist revolutions in Latin America, however, are less certain than in Asia and Africa, owing to the stake that the United States has in maintaining private enterprise throughout the Americas, with the economic and military power to back up its desires. After establishing itself in Cuba over twenty years ago, Marxism has recently found its way back to the Caribbean, and it also has made some progress for the first time in Central America. Marxist-Leninist parties and guerrilla units also exist in South America. However, it is so strongly in the interest of the United States to prevent the spread of the Marxist poison in the Western Hemisphere that the future success of such revolutions must be quite doubtful. Moreover, even if Marxist-Leninist revolutions do triumph here and there, U.S. economic power is likely to be exerted to prevent the success of the subsequent efforts at socialist economic development. If socialist development can be subverted, not only would those revolutions be endangered, but later revolutionary movements in the Americas would have to overcome the additional handicap of not being able to fulfill their promises after the revolution. The determination of the United States to turn back all threats to capitalism might even succeed, before too long, in reversing the revolutions in Cuba and Nicaragua.

Thus, the Americas are likely to remain capitalist for some time to come. However, capitalism can take any of several forms—liberal, dictatorial, militaristic, fascist, and so on. It is possible that each form will find a niche somewhere in the Western Hemisphere.

Love and Thermonuclear War

Jonathan Schell's best-selling book, *The Fate of the Earth,* was published in 1982. The theses of the book can be summarized as follows:

> A nuclear holocaust would annihilate us.
> It would also annihilate unborn generations.
> So let us love one another!

A nuclear holocaust would also annihilate all of the arguments of this book, all of the speculations, all of the predictions, timid and bold. Will loving one another save the day?

It probably would. But where is all that love going to come from? Schell supposes that the elimination of nation-states, and hence of superpower rivalry, would open the floodgates for an outpouring of love. But he does not inquire into the causes of nation-states, into whether those forces are becoming stronger or weaker. Nor does he investigate the history of the economic and class bases of the rivalry between the Soviet Union and the United States, between armed communism and armed capitalism.

We would all be more capable of loving one another if the world were entirely capitalist or entirely communist. Even then, we would probably have to contend with the burning heat of nationalism, the zealousness of religion, the animosity of racism, the dissonance of inequalities. But even without considering these other sources of friction, the arguments of this book have offered no more than a faint hope that the future is entirely in the hands of either capitalism or communism. Both systems have grave internal weaknesses, and each has served to enfeeble the other. When two wounded giants face each other, each armed to the teeth, it is fairly certain that love will be in short supply.

A continuing theme of this book is that contentious disunity is the prominent feature of the three worlds: of capitalism, communism, and the less-developed countries. A growing disunity is all too evident in the nuclear weapons arena too, as evidenced in the U.S. intelligence finding of November 1982 that "thirty-one countries, many of them engaged in long-standing regional disputes, will be able to produce nuclear weapons by the year 2000." It is not simply a question, then, of whether the Soviet Union and the United States can stare each other down through a maze of missiles, for a nuclear holocaust might be sparked in the future in any number of ways and from many directions.

So much disunity demands efforts for reunification. We have just noted the possibilities of some such endeavors—closer relations between the Soviet Union and China, the capitalist unification of the Americas, and a reunification of Europe. These and similar efforts will undoubtedly continue, at local, national, and international levels. But if the arguments of this book are correct, contentious disunities are more likely to be characteristic of the world to come than are concords of love.

The world's social movement is not so set as to make useless our efforts to overcome the many sources of dissension. To work for that outcome in a disruptive world may be more rewarding than to strive for nuclear arms limitations in the world as it presently is. If harmonies can overcome dissensions, love may yet emerge.

READER'S GUIDE

I OFFER ONLY A FEW WORKS of exceptional or timely interest to any readers of this book who now crave to learn more. Each of the following works will lead readers on to still other books of interest.

Chapters 1 and 2

A good start toward understanding Marxism-Leninism can be made by reading Marx's and Lenin's own works. The following two are especially rewarding:

- Marx, Karl and Engels, Friedrich. *The Communist Manifesto.* Arlington Heights, Illinois: AHM Publishing Corporation, 1955.
- Lenin, V. I. *Imperialism: The Highest Stage of Capitalism.* New York: International Publishers, 1939.

This is an outstanding introduction to the topic. It explains the theories and practices of Marx, Lenin, Stalin, and other communist leaders, and it applies these views to the contemporary communist scene:

- Meyer, Alfred G. *Communism.* New York: Random House, 1967.

Chapter 3

This work covers not only Marxism and the related communist movements, but also treats the many radical movements that competed with Marxism:

- Lichtheim, George. *Marxism: An Historical and Critical Study.* New York: Praeger Publishers, 1971.

These essays address the question of why socialism and Marxism never struck deep roots in the United States. The essays are accompanied by comments of critics and replies of authors:

- Laslett, John H. M. and Lipset, Seymour Martin (editors). *Failure of a Dream? Essays in the History of American Socialism.* New York: Anchor Press, 1974.

Chapter 4

This biographical history of Lenin, Stalin, and Trotsky explains clearly how and why Marxism made its way into Russia:

- Wolfe, Bertram D. *Three Who Made a Revolution.* New York: Dell Publishing Co., Inc., 1964.

This volume is indispensable for an understanding of why Marxism-Leninism became such a powerful ideology among China's peasants. An earlier, companion volume by Chesneaux and his associates, which covers China from the opium wars (1840s and 1850s) to the 1911 revolution, is well worth studying:

- Chesneaux, Jean; Le Barbier, Francoise; and Bergere, Marie-Claire. *China From the 1911 Revolution to Liberation.* New York: Pantheon Books, 1977.

Chapter 5

This volume presents an exceptionally clear explanation of the recent problems encountered by the U.S. economy. The author's solutions flow from his lucid explanations:

- Solomon, Ezra. *Beyond the Turning Point: The U.S. Economy in the 1980s.* Stanford: Stanford Alumni Association (The Portable Stanford), 1981, and San Francisco: W.H. Freeman, 1982.

Chapter 6

These volumes contain essays by experts on China, the Soviet Union, and Eastern Europe. The essays analyze all major aspects of these economies, and they present a wealth of quantitative material not easily available elsewhere:

- Joint Economic Committee, Congress of the United States. *Chinese Economy Post-Mao.* Two volumes. Washington, D.C.: U.S. Government Printing Office, 1978 and 1982.
- Joint Economic Committee, Congress of the United States. *Soviet Economy in a Time of Change.* Two volumes. Washington, D.C.: U.S. Government Printing Office, 1979.
- Joint Economic Committee, Congress of the United States. *East European Economic Assessment.* Two volumes. Washington, D.C.: U.S. Government Printing Office, 1981.

Chapter 7

The author of the following volume was a member of the Communist party in East Germany. Soon after the publication of this book in West Germany, he was arrested and charged with being a West German spy.

He was sentenced to eight years' imprisonment but was freed in October 1979 after an international campaign for his release. The book is a profound critique of the existing systems in Eastern Europe, and the author's alternative is democratic socialism:

- Bahro, Rudolf. *The Alternative in Eastern Europe.* London: Verso Edition, 1981. (Distributed by Schocken Books, New York.)

This offers a most valuable postwar history of workers' revolts in Poland and other Eastern European countries, which led to the Solidarity trade-union movement in Poland during 1980 and 1981. The author has a good understanding of Marxism-Leninism and of Polish history:

- Ascherson, Neal. *The Polish August.* London: Penguin Books, 1981.

This is a study of the Third World which views militarism as a necessary and beneficial means of achieving the stability necessary for both economic growth and the transition to democracy:

- Horowitz, Irving Louis. *Beyond Empire and Revolution.* Oxford and New York: Oxford University Press, 1982.

This book consists of essays on the newly emerging communist countries of Asia, Africa, and Latin America. It covers Vietnam, Ethiopia, Angola, Mozambique, and others. The essays are not of exceptional quality, but they are certainly timely:

- Wiles, Peter (editor). *The New Communist Third World.* New York: St. Martin's Press, 1982.

The author develops the theme that Britain—and perhaps other major capitalist countries—can no longer legislate coherent programs because society has become divided into too many contending factions:

- Beer, Samuel H. *Britain Against Itself.* New York: W. W. Norton & Co., 1982.

CREDITS

COVER   Cover design by Mark Olson.

CHARTS   The charts on pages 12, 23, and 109 are by Donna Salmon, Vallejo, California.

POSTERS   Special thanks to Carol Leadenham and Charles Palm of the Hoover Institution Archives at Stanford University, Stanford, California, for their assistance in researching the Hoover Institution's vast poster collections. The posters from the Hoover collections were photographed by Keith Jantzen and Robert Isaacs.

Photo: Stanford News and Publications

ABOUT THE AUTHOR

JOHN GURLEY'S association with Stanford is long and varied. He was an undergraduate economics major (Class of 1942) and a varsity tennis player. He also did his graduate work at Stanford and was an instructor in economics during 1949–50 while working on his doctorate. Having left Stanford during the 1950s, Gurley returned in 1961 as professor of economics, a position he still holds. He has taught twice at the Stanford campus in Tours, France. Over the years he has addressed many alumni groups; in 1975 and 1979 he was Dean of the Summer Alumni College; in 1975 he wrote *Challengers to Capitalism: Marx, Lenin, and Mao* for The Portable Stanford series; in 1978 he and his wife, Yvette, led an alumni tour group to China; in 1981 and 1982 he taught in the Stanford Executive Program in the Humanities; and he has participated in other summer programs for the Alumni Association.

From 1950 to 1953 Gurley taught economics at Princeton and from 1954 to 1961 was associate professor and professor at the University of Maryland while also serving as a senior staff member of the Brookings Institution. From 1963 through 1968 he was managing editor of the *American Economic Review,* the official publication of the American Economic Association; he was vice-president of that association in 1974. He presented the Alfred Marshall lectures at Cambridge University in the autumn of 1976.

Professor Gurley teaches several hundred undergraduates a year in his courses that range from elementary economics and money and banking to Marxian economic theory and Chinese economic development. He was the initial recipient in 1971 of the Walter J. Gores Award for excellence in teaching. He has been selected as one of the Class Day speakers by the Stanford senior class five times.

In odd hours, Gurley reports, he "serves and rushes the net, earns money on the side for opera tickets, runs the oval at Angell Field each day, and goes after mealy bugs, aphids, and snails in the garden."

INDEX

and religion, 129–130
Capitalist countries, 11, 12–13, 80–101, 105, 124, 135–142, 143, 165–166. *See also individual countries*
  disunity in, 90–101 *passim*, 135, 140–142, 151, 167
  economic growth in, 7, 72, 99, 119, 120, 123, 125, 135, 136, 137, 153, 159, 160, 163
  leading social classes of. *See* Capital-owning classes
  living standards in, 115, 116, 159
  Marxism in, 3, 165–166
  revolution expected in, 3, 6, 103
Capital-owning (and managing) classes, 18–26 *passim*, 37, 79, 124–142 *passim*, 160, 161
  Bellamy and, 57, 58
  and business cycles, 5, 58–59, 79, 101
  in communist countries, 111, 149
  and disunity, 90, 93, 98, 99, 135–136, 142
  exploitation of workers by, 4, 5, 7, 36, 38, 47, 55
  and income distribution, 25–26, 99
  Marxist revolution against, 7–9, 23, 31, 48
  reformists and, 45, 46
Caribbean, 66, 86–87, 159, 160, 165. *See also* Cuba
Cartel inflation, 94, 95
Castro, Fidel, 10, 66
Catholic Church, 153, 158
Catholic convictions, 128–129
Central America, 66, 86–87, 165. *See also individual countries*
Central Guild Congress, 43–44
Central Intelligence Agency, U.S., 53, 115
Central planning, 24–25, 28, 56, 104, 105, 106, 112, 113–114, 115
  in Mozambique, 119
  in Poland, 150
  reforms in, 146–149, 150, 158
  in Soviet bloc countries, 122–123, 145, 146, 148–149
  in Stalinist model, 144, 145–146
Chad, 159, 160
Chartism, 35–36, 48
Chenery, Hollis, 115
Chiang Kai-shek, 72–74, 75, 76
Chile, 159
China, 2, 11, 41, 61–76 *passim*, 107–117 *passim*
  and Albania, 122
  Cultural Revolution in, 107, 123
  economic development in, 3, 10, 74–75, 114–115, 117, 123, 143, 144, 148, 149

prerevolutionary, 71, 72–75, 76, 86
  revolution in, 6, 61, 66, 70–76, 77, 87
  socialism in, 27, 28, 29, 110, 112, 113, 149
  and Soviet Union, 2, 163–165, 167
  and Third World, 12, 161⁻
  worker revolts in, 150, 158
Ch'ing dynasty, 71, 72, 74, 75
Christianity, 43
Church, 38, 130, 153, 158
CIA, 53, 115
Civil rights legislation, 56. *See also* Human rights
Class consciousness, 6, 128
Class struggles, 21
  in capitalist countries, 6
  and nationalism, 128
  Poland and, 158
  syndicalists and, 43
  U.S. and, 49, 58
Classes, 21, 117, 124, 166. *See also* Capital-owning classes; Working classes
  in China, 75
  in less-developed countries, 7–9, 66–67, 159, 160, 165
  in Marxist socialism, 4, 26–27, 42, 63, 104, 114
  ruling, 9, 20–21, 23–24, 49, 66–67, 68, 111, 165
  in United States, 49, 58
Classical economics, 18, 20
Coal, 145
Coffee prices, 119
Collectivism. *See also* Cooperatives
  in agriculture, 29, 123, 144, 145, 148
  feudalism and, 49
  guild socialism and, 43, 48
  and less-developed Marxist countries, 105, 106
  U.S. and, 49, 58
Colonialism, 63, 66–67, 77, 86–87. *See also* Imperialism
  in less-developed communist countries, 117, 119, 120–122, 142
  and nationalism, 128
  and Third World, 13, 87, 88, 128, 129, 159, 165
Combined strategy, 113–114
Committee for the Defense of Workers' Rights (KOR), 153, 154
Communications systems, 46, 126
Communism, 1–142 *passim*, 165, 166, 167
Communist countries, 3, 4, 11, 12, 61–77, 100, 105–125, 132–161 *passim*. *See also individual countries*
  disunity in, 2, 150–151, 167

food prices in, 150
living standards in, 116
revolutions in, 64, 66, 68
socialism in, 56, 108, 112, 113, 143, 162, 163
and World War II, 76
East Germany, 143, 146, 149, 158
Economic base, defined, 21–23
Economic determinism, 45
Economic growth/development. *See also*
    Planning; Production
  in capitalist countries (general), 7, 72, 99, 110, 120, 123, 125, 135, 136, 137, 153, 159, 160, 163
  in China, 3, 10, 74–75, 114–115, 117, 123, 143, 144, 148, 149
  in communist countries (general), 1, 10, 103–125, 132–133, 142–143, 144, 147, 148, 156, 158–159
  in Poland, 123, 149, 150, 151–153, 158
  of Soviet Union, 1, 2–3, 110–117 *passim*, 122, 123, 143–149 *passim*
  in Third World, 7, 66–67, 159–160, 165
  in U.S., 90–94, 98, 100, 114–115, 135
Economic markets, 98, 99, 105
Economics, 53–55. *See also* Capitalism;
    Communism; Socialism
  Chartism and, 35–36
  classical, 18, 20
  Proudhonism and, 38
  syndicalists and, 42
Education, 116
Egypt, 160
Employers' organizations, 46
Employment levels, 89, 94, 100. *See also*
    Unemployment levels
Energy prices, 95, 120. *See also* Oil prices
Engels, Friedrich, 4, 46, 51, 61–63, 79, 117
  biography of, 17
  and capitalism to socialism transition, 6, 9, 17, 61–63, 66, 103–104, 106
  and German Social Democracy, 45
  Lenin and, 6, 9
  and production mode, 116
  and socialism to communism transition, 3, 104
  and utopians, 34
England, 45–46, 67, 131. *See also* Great
    Britain
Enlightenment, 16, 17–18
Entitlements, 97, 98–99, 100, 137–138
Environmentalists, 90, 93, 97, 137
Equality, 25–26, 38
Erfurt Programme, 45
Espionage Act, U.S., 53
Ethiopia, 86, 120, 122
Europe, 3, 20, 40, 52–53, 62–63, 70, 167.

See also Eastern Europe; Western Europe; *individual countries*
  and imperialism, 74, 86
  nationalism in, 126
  Russian Westernists and, 69
  social-security programs in, 138
  workers' organizations in, 32, 42
Evolutionary Socialism (Marx), 46
Exclusion Bill, Bismarck's, 44
Expenditures, government, 83, 92–93, 97, 98, 100, 138
Exploitation
  of consumer, 38
  and imperialism, 2, 6, 7
  of labor, 4, 5, 7, 36, 47, 55, 74–75

Fabians, 35, 45–46, 47
Factionalism, in American socialism, 51–52
Failure of a Dream? (Tyler), 51
Fate of the Earth, The (Schell), 166
FBI, 53
Feshbach, Murray, 116
Feudalism, 107, 111, 128
  capitalism following, 4, 15
  income distribution under, 27
  and planning, 24–25
  U.S. absence of, 49, 58
Financial disorders, 46, 53–56, 58. *See also*
    Banking; Cycles, business; Monetary
    systems
First World, 11, 12–13, 135–142. *See also*
    Capitalist countries
  capitalist class of, 136, 137–140, 142, 160, 161
  economic growth of, 135, 136, 137, 159, 160
  and imperialism, 87
Food, 74, 119, 120, 145, 150–151, 153. *See*
    also Agriculture
Foreign capitalists. *See also* Imperialism
  in nineteenth century, 7, 9, 35, 66–67, 70–71
  in twentieth century, 2, 80, 87, 89, 93, 148
Formosa, 72, 87
Fourier, Charles, 16, 33–34
Fourth World, 11, 12
France, 35, 80, 83, 90, 139, 183
  Blanc in, 16
  French Revolution in, 18, 20
  and human rights, 131
  and imperialism, 70–71, 72, 77, 86
  Industrial Revolution in, 18
  Marxism in, 3, 32, 66, 140
  Proudhon and, 38
  syndicalism in, 42

Marx, Karl (*Continued*)
  and income distribution, 25–26
  and International Workingmen's Association, 31, 38–40, 41
  and Lassalle, 36, 37
  Lenin and, 6, 7, 9
  and ownership of means of production, 24, 25–26
  and productive forces, 17, 23, 26, 117, 123
  and proletarianization, 83
  Proudhon and, 37, 38
  and socialism to communism transition, 3, 42, 104
  and surplus value, 5, 7, 47
Marxism, 1–142 *passim*, 165, 166, 167
Marxism-Leninism, 70, 122, 161–162, 164, 165–166
Materialist conception of history, 4, 21, 23, 26, 61
McCarthy attacks, 53
Meat, 150, 151, 153
Medicare, 56
Mediterranean immigrants, 89
Mercantilism, 126–128. *See also* Trade
Mexico, 67
Microplanning, 25, 104, 147
Middle classes. *See* Capital-owning classes
Military, 100, 114, 144, 145
  Chinese, 71
  Soviet, 2, 88, 122, 145, 167
  U.S., 1, 2, 137
Military regimes, 107, 156, 159, 161
Mill, James, 20
Mining, Chinese, 71
Ministerial planning system, 146
Mitterand government, 139, 163
Modernization, 126–128
Monarchies, 126–128, 130
Monetary systems, 55, 56, 97, 100
Mongolia, 11, 64, 66, 116, 143
Monopoly capitalism, 6, 7, 35, 70, 81
Morocco, 159, 160
Mozambique, 77, 119–120

Napoleonic wars, 128
Nationalism, 126–128, 166
  Chinese, 72, 74
  and imperialism, 67, 128, 129, 135
  Lenin and, 9
Nationalist party, in China, 72–74, 76
Nationalization
  of industries. *See* Ownership of means of production, social
  of Marxism, 128
National planning. *See* Central planning
National workshops, 16, 36

Nation-states, 126–128, 130–131, 166
Neocolonialism, 2, 93, 159, 165. *See also* Imperialism
Netherlands, 35, 83, 86, 138
New Communist Third World, The (Zafiris), 119
New Deal, 56
New Economic Mechanism (NEM), 147
New York Stock Exchange, 78, 91
New York *Tribune,* 34
New Zealand, 11, 84, 140
Nicaragua, 77, 120, 137, 166
Niger, 159
Nigeria, 159, 160
Noncommunist less-developed nations. *See* Third World
Nonsocialism, 124, 133, 142–143
North, the, 11
North America, 6, 9, 11, 62–63, 80, 140. *See also* Canada; United States
Northern Ireland, 159
North Korea, 11, 158
  economic development in, 10, 114, 117, 123, 143
  and World War II, 76
Norway, 138
Nuclear weapons, 2, 88, 167

O'Connor, Feargus, 36
Oil prices, 93, 94, 119, 123, 153
Oil-producing-and-exporting countries, 11, 12, 88, 93, 95, 135, 160
OPEC, 12, 88, 93, 95, 160
Opium trade, 71
Opium Wars, 71
Organization for Economic Cooperation and Development (OECD), 90
Organization of Petroleum Exporting Countries (OPEC), 12, 88, 93, 95, 160
Organization of Work (Blanc), 16
Owen, Robert, 15, 16
Ownership of means of production
  government, 81
  government-business partnership in, 139, 142
  private, 9, 24, 25–26, 27, 80–81, 82–83, 104. *See also* Capital-owning classes
  social, 15, 17, 24–28 *passim*, 35, 36, 56, 104, 105, 106, 115, 119, 123, 128, 144, 145, 149

Pacifism, 53
Pakistan, 159
Palmer raids, 53
Panama, 159
Paris Commune, 38, 79
Parliament, 43

workers' revolts in, 150, 158, 162
Spain, 35, 38, 40, 41, 87, 163
Spartacist revolt, 68
Stagflation, 94, 95, 98, 99, 101, 136
Stagnation, 101
Stalin, Joseph, 29
  and economic development, 10, 110,
    111, 143, 144–146, 150
  and socialism to communism transition,
    28
State, 35. *See also* Government
  anarchists and, 38, 40, 41–42, 43, 48
  bureaucratic party-dominated, 107–108,
    124, 142, 143, 144, 158–159
  guild socialists and, 43
  Lassalle and, 16–17, 35, 36–37
  Marxism and, 20, 35, 37, 56, 63
  monopoly capitalism of, 81
  nation-, 126–128, 130–131, 166
Steel, 145
Stock market, 78, 91, 92
Strikes, 42, 43, 151, 153–154, 155, 156
Students' Solidarity Committee, 153
Sun Yat-sen, 71–72
Superprofits, 7
Superstructures, 21, 23, 26, 117, 123–124
Supplies
  in capitalist systems, 89, 94, 95–97, 100
  in communist countries, 115, 122, 145
Supply-side programs, 101
Surplus incomes, 47
Surplus value, 5, 7, 47
Sweden, 83, 163
Sweezy, Paul, 32
Switzerland, 38, 83, 84
Sylvis, William, 55–56
Syndicalism, 35, 37, 40, 41, 42–43, 48

Taiping rebellion, 74
Taiwan, 160, 164
Taoism, 75
Taxes, 88, 95–100 *passim*, 137
Tax shelters, 137
Technological advances, 18–20, 28, 84
Territorial planning system, 146
Thailand, 160
Thatcher programs, 86, 137, 140
Theory. *See* Marxism; Marxism-Leninism
Third World, 11, 12, 100, 101, 135, 159–162
  capitalism's strengths in, 125–132, 133,
    165–166
  and colonialism, 7, 13, 87, 88, 128, 129,
    159, 165
  depressions and, 125
  disunity in, 167
  industry in, 119

living standards in, 115, 116, 159,
  161–162
Marxist-Leninist strength in, 6, 7–9, 61–
  70 *passim*, 161–162, 165–166
Thompson, William, 25
Tito (Josip Broz), 147–148
Tkachev, Petr, 61–62
Togliatti, Palmiro, 41
Tokugawa regime, 72
Trade, 87, 126, 137, 138–139. *See also* For-
  eign capitalists
  business cycles and, 125
  China and, 71
  Czechs and, 29
  Poland and, 150
Trade unions
  in capitalist countries, 35, 38, 42, 46, 51,
    53, 81, 82, 83
  in Poland, 138, 150, 151, 153, 154–156,
    158
  Sylvis and, 55–56
  syndicalism and, 42–43, 48
Transportation, Chinese, 71
Trotsky, Leon, 27–28, 49, 72, 110
Turkey, 159
Tyler, Gus, 51

Uganda, 160
Ulyanov, Vladimir Ilyich. *See* Lenin
Unemployment levels
  in capitalist countries, 89, 90, 91, 92, 94,
    95, 130
  in communist countries, 147
Unger, Irwin, 55
Unions. *See* Trade unions
United Kingdom. *See* Great Britain
United States, 12, 70–100 *passim*, 135–142
    passim, 162–167 *passim*
  and Cuba, 77, 116, 122, 166
  economic growth in, 90–94, 98, 100,
    114–115, 135
  and human rights, 131
  Industrial Revolution in, 18
  living standards in, 116
  Marxism (and socialism) in, 3, 32, 48–59,
    125
  military of, 1, 2, 137
  and nationalism, 128
  syndicalism in, 42
  and Vietnam, 64–66, 93, 95
Upper Volta, 160
Utopianism, 16, 33–35, 40, 48, 72

Venable, Vernon, 132
Versailles peace terms, 68